Psalms, Hymns and Spiritual Songs

Imprint:

Media Owner / Place of Publication: Markus Pilz, Schildlehen 35 / Vorberg 38, 8972 Ramsau am Dachstein

Manufacturer: Amazon Kindle-Direct Publishing (KDP), Amazon.com, Inc. and its affiliates

Place of Manufacture: see imprint on the last page

Bible-Translation: King James Version

Text, Melody and Design: The text of all hymns, the melody and the design and format of the hymn-book are in the Public Domain, no copyright

Melody

Suited for all hymns (the melody and all hymns are written in Common Meter – 8 6. 8 6 syllables)

1   **Psalm 1**

Blessed *is* the man that walketh / not in the counsel of / the ungodly, nor standeth in / the way of sinners, nor … sitteth in the seat of the scorn-ful. But his delight *is* / in the law of the LORD; in his / law doth he meditate … *both* day and night. And he shall be / like a tree planted *there* / by the rivers of water, that / bringeth forth his fruit in … his season; *and* his leaf also / shall not wither; and what-soever he doeth shall pros-per. The ungodly *are* … not so: but *are* like the chaff which / the wind driveth away. / Therefore the ungodly shall not / stand in the judgment, nor … sinners in the congregation / of the righteous. For the / LORD knoweth the way of the righ-teous: but the way of the … ungodly shall perish.

2 (1)   **Psalm 2**

Why do the heathen rage, and the / people imagine a / vain thing? The kings of the earth set / themselves, and the rulers … take counsel together, against / the LORD, and against his / anointed, *saying*, Let us break / their bands asunder, and … cast away their cords from us. He / that sitteth in the heav'ns / shall laugh: the LORD shall have them in / derision. Then shall he ... speak unto them in his wrath, and / vex them in his sore dis-pleasure. Yet have I set my king / upon my holy hill ... of Zion. I will declare the / decree: the LORD hath said / unto me, Thou *art* my Son; this / day have I begotten ... thee. Ask of me, and I shall give / *thee* the heathen *for* thine / inheritance, and the utter-most parts of the earth *for* ... thy possession. Thou shalt break them / with a rod of iron; / thou shalt dash them in pieces like / a potter's vessel. Be ... wise now therefore, O ye kings: be / instructed, ye judges / of the earth. Serve the LORD with fear, / and rejoice with trembling. ... Kiss the Son, lest he be angry, / and ye perish *from* the / way, when his wrath is kindled but / a little. Blessed *are* ... all they that put their trust in him.

2 (2)   Psalm 2

Why do the heathen rage, and the / people imagine a / vain thing? The kings of the earth set / themselves, and the rulers … take counsel together, against / the LORD, and against his / anointed, *saying*, Let us break / their bands asunder, and … cast away their cords from us. He / that sitteth in the heav'ns / shall laugh: the Lord shall have them in / derision. Then shall he … speak unto them in his wrath, and / vex them in his sore dis-pleasure. Yet have I set my king / upon my holy hill … of Zion. *Christ sitteth at my / right hand as the head of / the church.* I will declare the de-cree: the LORD hath said to … me, Thou *art* my Son; this day have / I begotten thee. Ask / me, I shall give *thee* the heathen / *for* thine inheritance, … and the uttermost parts of the / earth *for* thy possession. / Thou shalt break them with a rod of / iron; thou shalt dash them … in pieces like a potter's ves-sel. Be wise now therefore, / O ye kings: be instructed, ye / judges of the earth. Serve … the LORD with fear, and rejoice with / trembling. Kiss the Son, lest / he be angry, and ye perish / *from* the way, when his wrath … is kindled but a little. Bless'd / *are* all they that put their / trust in him. *Bless'd are all that put / their trust in Jesus Christ.*

3   Psalm 3

According to the Psalm of David, when he fled from Absalom his son.

LORD, how are they increased that trou-ble me! many are they / that rise up against me. Many / there be which say of my … soul, There is no help for him in / God. Interlude.
But thou, O LORD, art a shield for / me; my glory, and the / lifter up of mine head. I cried / unto the LORD with my … voice, and he heard me out of his / holy hill. Interlude.

I laid me down and slept; and I / awaked; for the LORD sus-tained me. I will not be afraid / of ten thousand people, ... that have set themselves against me / round about. Arise, O / LORD; save me, O my God: for thou / hast smitten all those mine ... enemies upon the cheek bone; / thou hast broken the teeth / of the ungodly. Salvation / belongeth unto the ... LORD: thy blessing is upon thy / people. Interlude.

4   Psalm 4

To the chief Musician on Neginoth, *According to the* Psalm of David.

Hear me when I call, O God of / my righteousness: thou hast / enlarged me *when I was* in dis-tress; have mercy upon ... me, and hear my pray'r. O ye sons / of men, how long *will ye / turn* my glory to shame? *how long* / will ye love vanity, ... *and* seek after leasing? Interlude.
But know that the LORD hath set a-part him that is godly / for himself: the LORD will hear when / I call unto him. Stand ... in awe, and sin not: commune with / your own heart upon your / bed, and be still. Interlude.
Offer the sacrifices of / righteousness, and put your / trust in the LORD. *There be* many / that say, Who will shew us ... *any* good? LORD, lift thou up the / light of thy countenance / upon us. Thou hast put gladness / in my heart, more than in ... the time *that* their corn and their wine / increased. I will both lay / me down in peace, and sleep: for thou, / LORD, only makest me ... dwell in safety.

5   **Psalm 5**

To the chief Musician upon Nehiloth, *According to the* Psalm of David.

Give ear to my words, O LORD, con-sider my medita-tion. Hearken unto the voice of / my cry, my King, and my ... God: for unto thee will I pray. / My voice shalt thou hear in / the morning, O LORD; in the mor-ning will I direct *my ... prayer* unto thee, and will look / up. For thou *art* not a / God that hath pleasure in wicked-ness: neither shall evil ... dwell with thee. The foolish shall not / stand in thy sight: thou hat'st / all workers of iniquity. / Thou shalt destroy them that ... speak leasing: the LORD will abhor / the bloody and deceit-ful man. But as for me, I will / come *into* thy house in ... the multitude of thy mercy: / *and* in thy fear will I / worship toward thy holy tem-ple. Lead me, O LORD, in ... thy righteousness because of mine / enemies; make thy way / straight before my face. For *there is* / no faithfulness in their ... mouth; their inward part *is* very / wickedness; their throat *is* / an open sepulchre; they flat-ter with their tongue. Destroy ... thou them, O God; let them fall by / their own counsels; cast them / out in the multitude of their / transgressions; for they have ... rebelled against thee. But let all / those that put their trust in / thee rejoice: let them ever shout / for joy, because thou wilt ... defend them: let them also that / love thy name be joyful / in thee. For thou, LORD, wilt bless the / righteous; with favour wilt ... thou compass him as *with* a shield.

6   **Psalm 6**

To the chief Musician on Neginoth upon Sheminith, *According to the* Psalm of David.

O LORD, rebuke me not in thine / anger, neither chasten / me in thy hot displeasure. Have / mercy upon me, O ... LORD; for I *am* weak: O LORD, heal / me; for my bones are vexed. / My soul too is sore vexed: but thou, / O LORD, how long? Return, ... O LORD, deliver my soul: oh / save me for thy mercies' / sake. For in death *there is* no re-membrance of thee: in the ... grave who shall give thee thanks? I am / weary with my groaning; / all the night make I my bed to / swim; I water my couch ... with my tears. Mine eye is consumed / because of grief; it wax'th / old because of all mine ene-mies. Depart from me, all ... ye workers of iniquity; / for the LORD hath heard the / voice of my weeping. The LORD hath / heard my supplication; ... the LORD will receive my prayer. / Let all mine enemies / be ashamed and sore vexed: let them / return *and let them* be ... ashamed suddenly.

7   **Psalm 7**

According to the Shiggaion of David, which he sang unto the LORD, concerning the words of Cush the Benjamite.

O LORD my God, in thee do I / put my trust: save me from / all them that persecute me, and / deliver me: Lest he … tear my soul like a lion, ren-ding *it* in pieces, while / *there is* none to deliver. O / LORD my God, if I have … done this; if there be iniqui-ty in my hands; If I / have rewarded evil unto / him that was at peace with … me; (yea, I have delivered him / that without cause is mine / enemy:) Let the enemy / persecute my soul, and … take *it*; yea, let him tread down my / life upon the earth, and / lay mine honour in the dust. Interlude. Arise, O LORD, in thine anger, / lift up thyself because / of the rage of mine enemies: / and awake for me *to* … the judgment *that* thou hast comman-ded. So shall the congre-gation of the people compass / thee about: for their sakes … therefore return thou on high. The / LORD shall judge the people: / judge me, O LORD, according to / my righteousness, and judge … me according to mine inte-grity *that is* in me. / Oh let the wickedness of the / wicked come to an end; … but establish the just: for the / righteous God trieth the / hearts and the reins. My defence *is* / of God, which saveth the … upright in heart. God judgeth the / righteous, God is

angry / *with the wicked* every day. If / he turn not, he will whet …
his sword; he hath bent his bow, and / made it ready. He hath / also
prepared for him the in-struments of death; and he … ordaineth his
arrows against / the persecutors. Be-hold, he travaileth with iniquity, and hath conceived … mischief, and brought forth falsehood.
He / made a pit, and digged it, / and is fallen into the ditch / *which*
he made. His mischief … shall return upon his own head, / and his
vi'lent dealing / shall come down upon his own pate. / I will praise
the LORD for … his righteousness: and will sing praise / to the
name of the LORD / most high.

8   **Psalm 8**

To the chief Musician upon Gittith, *According to the* Psalm of
David.

O LORD our Lord, how excellent / *is* thy name in all the / earth!
who hast set thy glory a-bove the heavens. Out of … the mouth of
babes and sucklings hast / thou ordained strength because / of thine
enemies, that thou might-est still the enemy … and the avenger.
When I con-sider thy heavens, the / work of thy fingers, the moon,
the / stars, which thou hast ordained; … What is man, that thou art
mindful / of him? and the son of / man, that thou visitest him? For /
thou hast made him a littl' … lower than the angels, and hast /
crowned him with glory and / honour. Thou madest him to have /
dominion over the … works of thy hands; thou hast put all / *things*
under his feet: All / sheep and oxen, yea, and the beasts / of the
field; The fowl of … the air, and the fish of the sea, / *and*
whatsoev'r passeth / through the paths of the seas. O LORD / our
Lord, how excellent … *is* thy name in all the earth!

9 (1)   **Psalm 9**

To the chief Musician upon Muth-labben, *According to the* Psalm of David.

I will praise *thee*, O LORD, with my / whole heart; I will shew forth / all thy marvellous works. I will / be glad and rejoice in … thee: I will sing praise to thy name, / O thou most High. When mine / enemies are turned back, they shall / fall and perish at thy … presence. For thou hast maintained my / right and my cause; thou sat'st / in the throne judging right. Thou hast / rebuked the heathen, thou … hast destroyed the wicked, thou hast / put out their name for ev'r / and ever. O thou enemy, / destructions are come to … a perpetual end: and thou / hast destroyed cities; their / memorial is perished with / them. But the LORD, he shall … endure for ever: he hath pre-pared his throne for judgment. / He shall judge the world in righteous-ness, he shall minister … judgment to the people in up-rightness. The LORD also / will be a refuge for the op-pressed, a refuge in times … of trouble. And they that know thy / name will put their trust in / thee: for thou, LORD, hast not forsa-ken them that seek thee. Sing … praises to the LORD, to him which / dwelleth there in Zion: / declare among the people his / doings. When he maketh … inquisition for blood, he re-memb'reth them: he forgett'th / not the cry of the humble. Have / mercy upon me, O … LORD; consider my trouble *which / I suffer* of them that / hate me, thou that liftest me up / from the gates of death: That … I may shew forth all thy praise in / the gates of the daughter / of Zion: I'll rejoice in thy / salvation. The heathen … are sunk down in the pit *that* they / made: in the net which they / hid is their own foot taken. The / LORD is known here by this … *by* the judgment *which* he exe-cuteth: the wicked is / snared in the work of his own hands. Interlude.
The wicked shall be turned into / hell, *and* all the nations / that forget God. For the needy, / they shall not alway be … forgotten: the expectation / of the poor shall *not* per-ish for ever. Arise, O LORD; /

let not man prevail: let … the heathen be judged in thy sight. / Put them *all* in fear, O / LORD: *so that* the nations may know / themselves *to be but* men. Interlude.

9 (2)   **Psalm 9**

I will praise thee, O LORD, with my / whole heart; I will shew forth / all thy marvellous works. I will / be glad and rejoice in … thee: I will sing praise to thy name, / O thou most High. For I / was sometimes darkness, but now I / am light in the Lord. My … understanding was darkened, but / now I walk as a child / of light. Thou hast saved me out of / the power of darkness, … thou art gracious and merciful / my LORD God and Saviour. / I was in time past a Gentile / in the flesh, yea, I was … uncircumcised, an alien / from the commonwealth of / Israel, and a stranger from / the cov'nants of promise, … and had no hope, and was without / God in the world. But now / I am made nigh by the blood of / Christ, I who sometimes was … far off, alienated from / the life of God through the / ignorance that was in me, be-cause of the blindness of … my heart. Christ hath destroyed the de-vil, and triumphed over / Satan on the cross spoiling prin-cipalities. I have … strived to enter in at the strait / gate, and have wrestled my-self through the narrow door to life. / The LORD also will be … a refuge for the sinner, a / refuge from judgment. And / they that know thy name will put their / trust in thee: for thou, LORD, … hast not forsaken them that seek / thee. Sing praises to the / LORD, which dwelleth in the church: de-clare among the people … his gospel. He forgetteth not / the cry of the afflict'd / and sinner. Have mercy upon / me, O LORD; consider … my battles, thou that liftest me / up from the gates of hell: / That I may shew forth all thy praise / there in the gates of the … heavenly Jerusalem in / the gates of thy church: I / will rejoice in thy salvation. / The devils are sunk down … in the pit that they made: in the / net which they hid is their / own foot taken. The LORD is known / by the judgment which he … executeth. Interlude.

The devils shall be turned into / hell, and all the nations / that forget God. For the needy, / they shall not alway be … forgotten: the expectation / of the poor shall not pe-rish for ever. Arise, O LORD; / let not man prevail: let … the heathen be judged in thy sight. / Put them all in fear, O / LORD: so that the nations may know / themselves to be but men. Interlude.

10   Psalm 10

Why stand'st thou afar off, O LORD? / *why* hid'st thou *thyself* in / times of trouble? The wicked in / *his* pride doth persecute … the poor: let them be taken in / the devices that they / have imagined. For the wicked / boasteth *there* of his heart's … desire, and blesseth the co-vetous, *whom* the LORD a-bhorreth. The wicked, through the pride / of his countenance, will … not seek *after God*: God *is* not / in all his thoughts. His ways / are always grievous; thy judgments / *are* far above out of … his sight: *as for* all his ene-mies, he puffeth at them. / He hath said in his heart, I shall / not be moved: for *I shall* … never *be* in adversity. / His mouth is full of cur-sing and deceit and fraud: under / his tongue *is* mischief and … vanity. He sitteth in the / lurking places of the / villages: in the secret pla-ces doth he murder the …innocent: his eyes are privi-ly set against the poor. / He lieth in wait secretly / as a lion in his … den: he lieth in wait to catch / the poor: he doth catch the / poor, when he draweth him into / his net. He croucheth, *and* … humbleth himself, that the poor may / fall by his strong ones. He / hath said in his heart, God hath for-gotten: he hideth his … face; he will never see *it*. A-rise, O LORD; O God, lift / up thine hand: forget not the hum-ble. Wherefore doth he, the … wicked contemn God? he hath said / in his heart, Thou wilt not / require *it*. Thou hast seen *it*; / for thou behold'st mischief … and spite, to requite *it* with thy / hand: the poor committeth / himself to thee; thou art the hel-per of the fatherless. … Break thou the arm of the wicked / and the evil *man*: seek / out his wickedness *till* thou find / none. The LORD *is* King for … ever and ever: the heathen / are perished out of his / land.

LORD, thou hast heard the desi-re of the humble: thou … wilt prepare their heart, thou wilt cause / thine ear to hear: To judge / the fatherless and the oppressed, / that the man of the earth … may no more oppress.

11   **Psalm 11**

To the chief Musician, *According to the Psalm* of David.

In the LORD put I my trust: how / say ye to my soul, Flee / *as* a bird to your mountain? For, / lo, the wicked bend *their* … bow, they make ready their arrow / upon the string, that they / may privily shoot at the up-right in heart. *And* if the … foundations be destroyed, what can / the righteous do? The LORD / *is* in his holy temple, the / LORD'S throne *is* in heaven: … his eyes behold, his eyelids try, / the children of men. The / LORD tri'th the righteous: but the wick-ed and him that loveth … violence his soul hateth. U-pon the wicked he shall / rain snares, fire and brimstone, and / an horrible tempest: … *this shall be* the portion of their / cup. For the righteous LORD / loveth righteousness; his count'nance / doth behold the upright.

12   **Psalm 12**

To the chief Musician upon Sheminith, *According to the* Psalm of David.

Help, LORD; for the godly man ceas-eth; for the faithful fail / from among the children of men. / They *all* speak vanity … every one with his neighbour: *with* / flattering lips *and* with / a double heart do they speak. *But* / the LORD shall cut off all … flattering lips, *and* the tongue that / speaketh proud things: Who have / said, With our tongue will we prevail; / our lips *are* our own: … who *is* lord over us? For the / oppression of the poor, / for the sighing of the needy, /

now will I arise, saith … the LORD; I will set *him* in saf-ety *from him that* puffeth / at him. The words of the LORD *are* / pure words: *as* silver tried … in a furnace of earth, puri-fied seven times. Thou shalt / keep them, O LORD, thou shalt preserve / them from this gen'ration … for ever. The wicked walk on / every side, when the vi-lest men are exalted.

13   Psalm 13

To the chief Musician, *According to the Psalm* of David.

How long wilt thou forget me, O / LORD? for ever? how long / wilt thou hide thy face from me? How / long shall I take counsel … in my soul, *having* sorrow in / my heart daily? how long / shall mine enemy be exal-ted over me? Hear me … *and* consider, O LORD my God: / lighten mine eyes, lest I / sleep the *sleep of* death; Lest mine e-nemy say, *now* I have … prevailed against him; *and* those that / trouble me rejoice when / I am moved. But I have trusted / in thy mercy; my heart … shall rejoice in thy salvation. / I will sing unto the / LORD, because he hath dealt bounti-fully with me.

14   Psalm 14

To the chief Musician, *According to the Psalm* of David.

The fool hath said in his heart, *There / is* no God. They are cor-rupt, they have done abomina-ble works, *there is* none that … doth good. The LORD looked down from hea-ven upon the children / of men, to see if there were a-ny that did understand, … *and* seek God. They are all gone a-side, they are *all* togeth'r / become filthy: *there is* none that / doeth good, no, not one. … Have all the workers of ini-quity no knowledge? who / eat up my people *as* they eat / bread, and call not upon … *they* call not on the LORD. There were / they in great fear: for God / *is* in the generation of / the righteous. Ye have shamed … the counsel of the poor, because / the LORD *is* his refuge. / Oh that the salvation of Is-rael *were come* out of … Zion! when the LORD bringeth back / the captivity of / his people, Jacob shall rejoice, / *and* Isr'el shall be glad.

15   **Psalm 15**

According to the Psalm of David.

LORD, who shall abide in thy ta-bernacle? who shall dwell / in thy holy hill? He that wal-keth uprightly, and work'th … righteousness, and speaketh the truth / in his heart. *He that* back-biteth not with his tongue, nor doth / evil to his neighbour, … nor taketh up a reproach a-gainst his neighbour. In whose / eyes a vile person is contemned; / but he honoureth them … that fear the LORD. *He that* sweareth / to *his own* hurt, and chan-geth not. *He that* putteth not out / his money to us'ry, … nor taketh reward against the / innocent. He that doth / these *things* shall never be moved.

16   **Psalm 16**

According to the Michtam of David.

Preserve me, O God: for in thee / do I put my trust. *O / my soul,* thou hast said unto the / LORD, Thou *art* my Lord: my … goodness *extendeth* not to thee; / *But* to the saints that *are* / in the earth, and *to* the excel-lent, in whom *is* all my … delight. Their sorrows shall be mul-tiplied *that* hasten *af-ter* another *god*: their drink off'-rings of blood will I not … offer, nor take up their names in-to my lips. The LORD *is* / the portion of mine inheri-tance and of my cup: thou … maintainest my lot. The lines are / fallen unto me in / pleasant *places*; yea, I have a / goodly heritage. I … I will bless the LORD, who hath gi-ven me counsel: my reins / also instruct me in the night / seasons. I have set the … LORD always before me: because /

he is at my right hand, / I shall not be moved. Therefore my / heart is glad, my glory … rejoiceth: *and* my flesh also / shall rest in hope. For thou / wilt not leave my soul in hell; nei-ther wilt thou suffer thine … Holy One to see corruption. / Thou wilt shew me the path / of life: in thy presence *is* ful-ness of joy; at thy right … hand *there are* pleasures for ever-more.

17   **Psalm 17**

According to the Prayer of David.

Hear the right, O LORD, attend un-to my cry, give ear un-to my prayer, *that goeth* not / out of feigned lips. Let my … sentence come forth from thy presence; / let thine eyes behold the / things that are equal. Thou hast proved / mine heart; thou hast vis'ted … *me* in the night; thou hast tried me, / *and* shalt find nothing; I / am purposed *that* my mouth shall not / transgress. Concerning the … works of men, by the word of thy / lips I have kept *me from* / the paths of the destroyer. Hold / up my goings in thy … paths, *that* my footsteps slip not. I / have called upon thee, for / thou wilt hear me, O God: incline / thine ear unto me, *and* … *hear* my speech. Shew thy marvellous / lovingkindness, O thou / that savest by thy right hand them / which put their trust *in thee* … from those that rise up *against them.* / Keep me as the apple / of the eye, hide me under the / shadow of thy wings, From … the wicked that oppress me, *from* / my deadly enemies, / *who* compass me about. They are / inclosed in their own fat: … with their mouth they speak proudly. They / have now compassed us in / our steps: they have set their eyes bo-wing down to the earth; Like … as a lion *that* is greedy / of his prey, and as it / were a young lion lurking in / secret places. Arise, … O LORD, disappoint him, cast him / down: deliver my soul / from the wicked, *which is* thy sword: / From men *which are* thy hand, … O LORD, from men of the world, *which* / *have* their portion in *this* / life, and whose belly thou fillest / with thy hid *treasure*: they … are full of children, and leave the / rest of their *substance* to / their babes. As for me, I'll behold / thy face in righteousness: ... I shall be satisfied, when I / awake, with thy likeness.

18   **Psalm 18**

To the chief Musician, *According to the Psalm* of David, the servant of the LORD, who spake unto the LORD the words of this song in the day *that* the LORD delivered him from the hand of all his enemies, and from the hand of Saul: And he said,

I will love thee, O LORD, my strength. / The LORD *is* my rock, and / my fortress, and my delive-rer; my God, my strength, in ... whom I will trust; my buckler, and / the horn of my salva-tion, *and* my high tower. I will / call upon the LORD, *who ... is worthy* to be praised: so shall / I be saved from *those* mine / enemies. The sorrows of death / compassed me, and the floods ... of ungodly men made me a-fraid. The sorrows of hell / compassed me about: the snares of / death prevented me. In ... my distress I called upon the / LORD, and cried unto my / God: he heard my voice out of his / temple, and my cry came ... before him, *even* into his / ears. Then the earth shook and / trembled; the foundations also / of the hills moved and were ... shaken, because he was wroth. There / went up a smoke out of / his nostrils, and fire out of / his mouth devoured: coals ... were kindled by it. He bowed the / heavens also, and came / down: and darkness *was* under his / feet. And he rode upon ... a cherub, and did fly: yea, he / did fly upon the wings / of the wind. He made darkness his / secret place; his pav'lion ... round about him *were* dark waters / *and* thick clouds of the skies. / At the brightness *that was* before / him his thick clouds passed, hail ... *stones* and coals of fire. The LORD / also thundered in the / heavens, and the Highest gave his / voice; hail *stones* and coals of ... fire. Yea, he sent out his ar-rows, and scattered them; and / he shot out lightnings, and discom-fited them. *And* then the ... channels of waters were seen, and / the foundations of the / world were discovered at thy re-buke, O LORD, at the blast … of the breath of thy nostrils. He / sent from above, he took / me, he drew me out of many / waters. He delivered … me from my strong enemy, and / from them which hated me: / for they were too strong for me. They / prevented me in the … day of my calamity: but / the LORD was my stay. He / brought me forth also into a / large place; he delivered … me, because he delighted in / me. The LORD rewarded / me according to my righteous-ness; according to the … cleanness of my hands hath he re-compensed me. For I have / kept the ways of the LORD, and have / not wickedly depart'd … from my God. For all his judgments / *were* before me, and I / did not put away his statutes / from me. I was also / upright before him, and I kept / myself from mine ini-quity. Therefore hath the LORD re-compensed me according … to my righteousness, according / to the cleanness of my / hands in his eyesight. *For* with the / merciful thou wilt shew … thyself merciful; with an up-right man thou wilt shew thy-self upright; With the pure thou wilt / shew thyself pure; and with … the froward thou wilt shew thyself / froward. For thou wilt save / the afflicted people; but wilt / bring down high looks. For thou … wilt light my candle: the LORD my / God will enlighten my / darkness. For by thee I have run / through a troop; and by my … God have I leaped over a wall. / *As for* God, his way *is* / perfect: the word of the LORD is / tried: he *is* a buckler … to all those that trust in him. For / who *is* God save the LORD? / or who *is* a rock save our God? / *It is* God that girdeth … me with strength, and maketh my way / perfect. He maketh my / feet like hinds' *feet*, and setteth me / upon my high places. … He teacheth my hands to war, so / that a bow of steel is / broken by mine arms. Thou hast al-so given me the shield … of thy salvation: and thy right / hand hath holden me up, / and thy gentleness hath made me / great. Thou hast enlarged my … steps under me, that my feet did / not slip. I have pursued / mine enemies, and overta-ken them: neither did I … turn again till they were consumed. / I have wounded them that / they were not able to rise: they / are fallen under my … feet. For thou hast girded me with / strength unto the battle: / thou hast subdued under me those / that rose up against me. … Thou hast also given me the / necks of mine enemies; / that I might destroy them that hate / me. They cried, but *there was* … none to save *them: even* unto / the LORD, but he answered / them not. Then did I beat them small / as the dust before the … wind: I did cast them out as the / dirt in the streets. Thou hast / delivered me from the strivings / of the people; *and* thou … hast made me the head of the hea-then: a people *whom* I / have not known shall serve me. As soon / as they hear of me, they … shall obey me: the strangers shall / submit themselves unto / me. The strangers shall fade away, / and be afraid out of … their close places. The LORD liveth; / and blessed *be* my rock; / and let the God of my salva-tion be exalted. *It … is* God that avengeth me, and / subdueth the people / under me. He delivereth / me from mine enemies: … yea, thou liftest me up above / those that rise up against / me: thou hast delivered me from / the violent man. *And* … therefore will I give thanks unto / thee, O LORD, among the / heathen, and sing praises unto / thy name. Great deliv'rance … giveth he to his king; and shew-eth mercy to his a-nointed, to David, and to his / seed for evermore.

19   **Psalm 19**

To the chief Musician, *According to the* Psalm of David.

The heavens declare the glory / of God; and the firma-ment sheweth his handywork. Day / unto day uttereth … speech, and night unto night sheweth / knowledge. *There is* no speech / nor language, *where* their voice is not / heard. Their line is gone out … through all the earth, and their words to / the end of the world. In / them hath he set a taberna-cle for the sun, Which *is* … as a bridegroom coming out of / his chamber, *and* rejoi-ceth as a strong man to run a / race. His going forth *is* … from the end of the heaven, and / his circuit unto the / ends of it: and there is nothing / hid from the heat thereof. … The law of the LORD *is* perfect, / converting the soul: the / testimony of the LORD *is* / sure, *and* making wise the … simple.

The statutes of the LORD / *are* right, rejoicing the / heart: the commandment of the LORD / *is* pure, enlightening the … eyes. The fear of the LORD *is* clean, / enduring for ever: / the judgments of the LORD *are* true, / righteous altogether. … More to be desired *are they* / than gold, yea, than much fine / gold: sweeter also than honey / and *than* the honeycomb. … Moreover by them is thy ser-vant warned: *and* in keeping / of them *there is* great reward. Who / can understand *his* err'rs? … cleanse thou me from secret *faults*. Keep / back thy servant also / from presumptu's *sins*; let them not / have dominion over …me: then shall I be upright, and / I shall be innocent / from the great transgression. Let the / words of my mouth, and the … meditation of my heart, be / acceptable in thy / sight, O LORD, my strength, and my re-deemer.

20   Psalm 20

To the chief Musician, *According to the* Psalm of David.

The LORD hear thee in the day of / trouble; the name of the / God of Jacob defend thee; *And / he* send thee help from the ... sanctuary, and strengthen thee / out of Zion; Remem-ber all thy offerings, and ac-cept thy burnt sacrifice; Interlude.
Grant thee according to thine own / heart, and fulfil all thy / counsel. We will rejoice in thy / salvation, and in the ... name of our God we will set up / *o'r* banners: the LORD ful-fil all thy petitions. Now know / I that the LORD saveth ... his anointed; he will hear him / from his holy heaven / with the saving strength of his right / hand. Some *trust* in chariots, ... and some in horses: but we will / remember the name of / the LORD our God. They are brought down / and fallen: but we are ... risen, and stand upright. Save, LORD: / let the king hear us when / we call.

21   Psalm 21

To the chief Musician, *According to the* Psalm of David.

The king shall joy in thy strength, O / LORD; in thy salvation / how greatly shall he rejoice! Thou / hast given him his heart's ... desire, and hast not withhol-den the request of his / lips. Interlude.
For thou preventest him with the / blessings of goodness: thou / settest a crown of pure gold on / his head. He ask'd life of ... thee, *and* thou gavest *it* him, *e-ven* length of days for ev'r / and ever. *And* his glory *is* / great in thy salvation: ... honour and majesty hast thou / laid upon him. For thou / hast made him most blessed for e-ver: *and* thou hast made him ... exceeding glad with thy counte-nance. For the king trusteth / in the LORD, and through the mercy / of the most High he shall ... not be moved. Thine hand shall find out / all thine enemies: thy / right hand shall find out those that hate / thee. Thou shalt make them as ... a fi'ry oven in the time / of thine anger: the LORD / shall swallow them up in his wrath, / the fire shall devour ... them. Their fruit shalt thou destroy from / the earth, and their seed from / among the children of men. For / they intended evil ... against thee: they imagined a / mischievous device, *which* / they are not able *to perform.* / Therefore shalt thou make them ... turn their back, *when* thou shalt make rea-dy *thine arrows* upon / thy strings against the face of them. / Be thou exalted, LORD, ... in thine own strength: *so* will we sing / and praise thy power.

22   Psalm 22

To the chief Musician upon Aijeleth Shahar, *According to the* Psalm of David.

My God, my God, why hast thou for-saken me? *why art thou / so* far from helping me, *and from* / the words of my roaring? ... O my God, I cry in the day-time, but thou hearest not; / and in the night season, and am / not silent. But thou *art* ... holy, *O thou* that inhabi-test the praises of Is-rael. Our fathers trusted in / thee: they trusted, and thou ... didst deliver them. They cried un-to thee, and *they* were de-livered: they trusted in thee, and / were not confounded. But ... I *am* a worm, and no man; a / reproach of men, despised / of the people. All they that see / me laugh me to scorn: they ... shoot out the lip, they shake the head, / *saying*, He trusted on / the LORD *that* he would deliver / him: let him deliver ... him, seeing he delighted in / him. But thou *art* he that / took me out of the womb: thou didst / make me hope *when I was* ... upon my mother's breasts. I was / cast upon thee from the / womb: thou *art* my God from my mo-ther's belly. Be not far ... from me; for trouble *is* near; for / *there is* none to help. Ma-ny bulls have compassed me: strong *bulls* / of Bashan have beset ... me round. They gaped upon me *with* / their mouths, *as* a rav'ning / and a roaring lion. I am / poured out like water, and ... all my bones are out of joint: my / heart is like wax; it is / melted in the midst of my bow-els. My strength is dried up ... like a potsherd; and my tongue clea-veth to my jaws; and thou / hast brought me into the dust of / death. For dogs have compassed ... me: the assembly of the wick-ed have inclosed me: they / pierced my hands and my feet. I may / tell all my bones: they look ... *and* stare upon me. They part my / garments among them, and / cast lots upon my vesture. But / be not thou far from me, ... O LORD: O my strength, haste thee to / help me. Deliver my / soul from the sword; my darling from / the power of the dog. ... Save me from the lion's mouth: for / thou hast heard me from the / horns of the unicorns. I will / declare thy name unto ... my brethren: in the midst of the / congregation will I / praise thee. Ye that fear the LORD, praise / him; all ye the seed of ... Jacob, glorify him; fear him, / all ye the seed of Is-r'el. For he hath not despised nor / abhorred the affliction ... of the afflicted; neither hath / he hid his face from him; / but when he cried unto him, he / heard. My praise *shall be* of ... thee in the great congregation: / I'll pay my vows before / them that fear him. The meek shall eat / and be satisfied: they ... shall praise the LORD that seek him: your / heart shall live for ever. / All the ends of the world shall re-member and turn unto ... the LORD: and all the

kindreds of / the nations shall worship / before thee. For the
kingdom *is* / the LORD'S: and he *is* the ... governor among the
nations. / All *they that be* fat on / earth shall eat and worship: all
they / that go down to the dust ... shall bow before him: and none
can / keep alive his own soul. / A seed shall serve him; it shall be /
accounted to the Lord ... for a generation. They shall / come, and
shall declare his / righteousness unto a people / that shall be born,
that he ... hath done *this*.

23   Psalm 23

According to the Psalm of David.

The LORD *is* my shepherd; I shall / not want. He maketh me / to lie
down in green pastures: he / leadeth me beside the ... still waters. He
restoreth my / soul: he leadeth me in / the paths of righteousness for
his / name's sake. Yea, though I walk … through the valley of the
shadow / of death, I will fear no / evil: for thou *art* with me; *and* /
thy rod and thy staff they … comfort me. Thou preparest a / table
before me in / the presence of mine enemies: / thou anointest my
head … with oil; *and* my cup runneth o-ver. Surely goodness and /
mercy shall follow me all the / days of my life: and I … will dwell
in the house of the LORD / for ever.

24   Psalm 24

According to the Psalm of David.

The earth *is* the LORD'S, and the ful-ness thereof; the world, and /
they that dwell therein. For he hath / founded it upon the … seas,
and established it upon / the floods. Who shall ascend / into the hill
of the LORD? or / who shall stand *there* in his … holy place? He
that hath clean hands, / and a pure heart; who hath / not lifted up his
soul unto / vanity, nor *who hath* … sworn deceitfully. He shall re-

ceive the blessing from the / LORD, and righteousness from the God / of his salvation. This ... *is* the generation of them / that seek him, that seek thy / face, O Jacob. Interlude.

Lift up your heads, O ye gates; be / ye lift up, ye ever-lasting doors; and the King of glo-ry shall come in. Who *is* ... this King of glory? The LORD strong / and mighty, *yea*, the LORD / mighty in battle. Lift up your / heads, O ye gates; even ... lift *them* up, O ye everlas-ting doors; and the King of / glory shall come in. Who is this / King of glory? The LORD ... of hosts, he *is* the King of glo-ry. Interlude.

25   Psalm 25

According to the Psalm of David.

Unto thee, O LORD, do I lift / up my soul. O my God, / I trust in thee: let me not be / ashamed, *and* let not mine ... enemies triumph over me. / Yea, let none that wait on / thee be ashamed: let them be a-shamed which transgress without ... cause. Shew me thy ways, O LORD; teach / me thy paths. Lead me in / thy truth, teach me: for thou *art* the / God of my salvation; ... on thee do I wait all the day. / Remember, O LORD, thy / tender mercies and thy loving-kindnesses; for they *have* ... *been* ever of old. Remember / not the sins of my youth, / nor my transgressions: according / to thy mercy *I plead* ... remember thou me for thy good-ness' sake, O LORD. Good and / upright *is* the LORD: therefore will / he teach sinners in the ... way. The meek will he guide in judg-ment: and the meek will he / teach his way. All the paths of the / LORD *are* mercy and truth ... to such as keep his covenant / and his testimonies. / For thy name's sake, O LORD, pardon / mine iniquity; for ... it *is* great. What man *is* he that / feareth the LORD? him shall / he teach in the way *that* he shall / choose. His soul shall dwell at ... ease; and his seed shall inherit / the earth. The secret of / the LORD *is* with them that fear him; / and he will shew them his ... covenant. Mine eyes *are* ever / toward the LORD; for he / shall pluck my feet out of the net. / Turn thee unto me, and ... have mercy upon me; for I / *am* desolate and af-flicted. The troubles of my heart / are enlarged: *O* bring thou … me out of my distresses. Look / upon mine affliction / and my pain; and forgive all my / sins. *And* consider mine … enemies; for they are many; / and they hate me with cruel / hatred. O keep my soul, and de-liver me: let me not … be ashamed; for I put my trust / in thee. Let integri-ty and uprightness preserve me; / because I wait on thee. … Redeem Israel, O God, out / of all his troubles.

26   Psalm 26

According to the Psalm of David.

Judge me, O LORD; for I have walked / in mine integrity: / I have trusted also in the / LORD; *therefore* I shall not … slide. Examine me, O LORD, and / prove me; try my reins and / my heart. For thy lovingkindness / *is* before mine eyes: and … I have walked in thy truth. I have / not sat with vain persons, / neither will I go in with dis-semblers. I have hated … the congregation of evil / doers; and will not sit / with the wicked. I will wash mine / hands in innocency: … so will I compass thine altar, / O LORD: So that I may / publish with the voice of thanksgi-ving, and tell of all thy … wondrous works. LORD, I have loved the / habitation of thy / house, and the place where thine honour / dwelleth. Gather not my … soul with sinners, nor my life with / bloody men: In whose hands / *is* mischief, and their right hand is / full of bribes. But as for … me, I will walk in mine inte-grity: redeem me, and / be merciful unto me. My / foot standeth in an ev'n … in an even place: in the con-gregations will I bless / the LORD.

According to the Psalm of David.

The LORD *is* my light and my sal-vation; whom shall I fear? / the LORD *is* the strength of my life; / of whom shall I be 'fraid? … When the wicked, *even* mine e-nemies and my foes, came / upon me to eat up my flesh, / they stumbled and fell. Though … an host should encamp against me, / my heart shall not fear: though / war should rise against me, in this / *will* I *be* confident. … One *thing* have I desired of / the LORD, that will I seek / after; that I may dwell in the / house of the LORD all the … days of my life, to behold the / beauty of the LORD, and / to inquire in his temple. / For *there* in the time of … trouble he shall *surely* hide me / in his pavilion: in / the secret of his taberna-cle shall he hide me; he … shall set me up upon a rock. / And now shall mine head be / lifted up above mine ene-mies round about me: *and* … therefore will I offer in his / tabernacle sacri-fices of joy; I will sing, yea, / I will sing praises to … the LORD. Hear, O LORD, *when* I cry / with my voice: have mercy / also upon me, and answer / me. *When thou saidst*, Seek ye … my face; my heart said unto thee, / Thy face, LORD, will I seek. / Hide not thy face *far* from me; put / not thy servant away … in anger: thou hast been my help; / leave me not, neither for-sake me, O God of my salva-tion. When my father and … my mother forsake me, then the / LORD will take me up. Teach / me thy way, O LORD, and lead me / in a plain path, because … of mine enemies. Deliver / me not over unto / the will of mine enemies: for / false witnesses are ris'n … up against me, and such as breathe / out cruelty. *I had / fainted*, unless I had believed / to see the goodness of … the LORD in the land of the li-ving. Wait on the LORD: be / of good courage, and he shall streng-then thine heart: wait, I say, … on the LORD.

28   Psalm 28

According to the Psalm of David.

Unto thee will I cry, O LORD / my rock; be not silent / to me: lest, *if* thou be silent / to me, I become like … them that go down into the pit. / *And* hear the voice of my / supplications, when I cry un-to thee, when I lift up … my hands t'ward thy holy ora-cle. Draw me not away / with the wicked, and with the wor-kers of iniquity, … which speak peace to their neighbours, but / mischief *is* in their hearts. / Give them according to their deeds, / and according to the … wickedness of their endeavours: / give them after the work / of their hands; render to them their / desert. Because they see, … they regard not the works of the / LORD, nor the opera-tion of his hands, he shall destroy / them, and not build them up. … Blessed *be* the LORD, because he / hath heard the voice of my / supplications. The LORD *is* my / strength and my shield; my heart … trusted in him, and I am helped: / therefore my heart greatly / rejoiceth; and with my song will / I praise him. The LORD *is* … their strength, and he *is* the saving / strength of his anointed. / Save thy people, and bless thine in-heritance: *and* feed them … also, and lift them up for e-ver.

29   Psalm 29

According to the Psalm of David.

Give unto the LORD, O ye migh-ty, give unto the LORD / glory and strength. Give unto the / LORD the glory due to … his name; worship the LORD in the / beauty of holiness. / The voice of the LORD *is* upon / the waters: the God of … glory thundereth: the LORD *is* / upon many waters. / The voice of the LORD *is* power-ful; the voice of the LORD … *is* full of majesty. The voice / of the LORD breaketh the / cedars; yea, the LORD breaketh the / cedars of Lebanon. … He maketh them also to skip / like a calf; Lebanon / and Sirion like a young u-nicorn. The voice of the … LORD divideth the flames of fire. / The voice of the LORD sha-keth the wilderness; the LORD sha-keth the wilderness of … Kadesh. The voice of the LORD ma-keth the hinds to calve, and / discovereth the forests: and / in his temple *there* doth … every one speak of *his* glory. / The LORD sitteth upon / the flood; yea, the LORD sitteth King / for ever. The LORD will …give strength unto his people; the / LORD will bless his people / with peace.

30   Psalm 30

According to the Psalm *and* Song *at* the dedication of the house of David.

I will extol thee, O LORD; for / thou hast lifted me up, / and hast not made my foes to re-joice over me. O LORD … my God, I cried unto thee, and / thou hast healed me. O LORD, / thou hast brought up my soul from the / grave: *and* thou hast kept me … alive, that I should not go down / to the pit. Sing unto / the LORD, ye saints of his, and give / thanks at the remembrance … of his holiness. For his an-ger *endureth but* a / moment; in his favour *is* life: / weeping may endure for … a night, but joy *cometh* in the / morning. And in my pros-perity I said, I shall ne-ver be moved. LORD, by thy … favour thou hast made my mountain / to stand strong: thou didst hide / thy face, *and* I was troubled. I / cried to thee, O LORD; and … unto the LORD I made suppli-cation. What profit *is* / *there* in my blood, when I go down / to the pit? Shall the dust … praise thee? shall it declare thy truth? / Hear, O LORD, have mercy / upon me: LORD, be thou my hel-per. Thou hast turned for me … my mourning into dancing: thou / hast put off my sackcloth, / and girded me with gladness; To / the end that *my* glory … may sing praise to thee, and not be / silent. O LORD my God, / I will give thanks unto thee for / ever.

31   Psalm 31

To the chief Musician, *According to the* Psalm of David.

In thee, O LORD, do I put my / trust; let me never be / ashamed: deliver me in thy / righteousness. Bow down thine … ear to me; deliver me spee-dily: be thou my strong / rock, for an house of defence to / save me. For thou *art* my … rock and my fortress; therefore for / thy name's sake lead me, and / guide me. Pull me out of the net / that they have laid priv'ly … for me: for thou *art* my strength. In-to thine hand I commit / my spirit: thou hast redeemed me, / O LORD God of truth. I … have hated them that regard ly-ing vanities: but I / trust in the LORD. *And* I will be / glad and rejoice in thy … mercy: for thou hast considered / my trouble; thou hast known / my soul in adversities; And / *thou* hast not shut me up … into the hand of the ene-my: thou hast set my feet / in a large room. Have mercy u-pon me, O LORD, for I … am in trouble: mine eye is con-sumed with grief, *yea*, my soul / and my belly. For my life is / spent with grief, and my years … with sighing: my strength faileth be-cause of mine in'quity, / and my bones are consumed. I was / a reproach among all … mine enemies, but 'specially / among my neighbours, and / a fear to mine acquaintance: they / that did see me without … fled from me. I am forgotten / as a dead man out of / mind: I am like a broken ves-sel. For I have heard the … slander of many: fear *was* on / every side: while they took / counsel together against me, / they devised to take 'way … my life. But I trusted in thee, / O LORD: I said, Thou *art* / my God. My times *are* in thy hand: / deliver me from the … hand of mine enemies, and from / them that persecute me. / Make thy face to shine upon thy / servant: save me for thy … mercies' sake. Let me not be a-shamed, O LORD; for I have / called upon thee: let the wicked / be ashamed, *and* let them … be silent in the grave. Let the / lying lips be put to / silence; which speak grievous things proud-ly and contemptuously … against the righteous. *Oh* how great / *is* thy goodness, which thou / hast laid up for them that fear thee; / *which* thou hast wrought for them … that trust in thee before the sons / of men! Thou shalt hide them / in the secret of thy presence / from the pride of man: thou … shalt keep them secretly in a / pavilion from the strife / of tongues. Bless'd *be* the LORD: for he / hath shewed me his marv'llous … kindness in a strong city. For / I said in my haste, I / am cut off from before thine eyes: / nevertheless thou heard'st … the voice of my supplications / when I cried unto thee. / O love the LORD, all ye his saints: / *for* the LORD preserveth … the faithful, and plentifully / rewardeth the proud do'r. / Be of good courage, and he shall / strengthen your heart, all ye … that hope in the LORD.

32   **Psalm 32**

According to the Psalm of David, Maschil.

Blessed *is he whose* transgression / *is* forgiven, *whose* sin / *is* covered. Bless'd *is* the man to / whom the LORD imputeth … not iniquity, and in whose / spirit *there is* no guile. / When I kept silence, my bones waxed / old through my roaring all … the day long. For day and night thy / hand was heavy upon / me: *and* my moisture is turned in-to the drought of summer. Interlude.
I acknowledged my sin to thee, / and mine iniquity / have I not hid. I said, I will / confess my transgressions … unto the LORD; and thou forga-vest the iniquity / of my sin. Interlude.
For this shall every one that is / godly pray unto thee / in a time when thou mayest be / found: surely in the floods … of great waters they shall not come / nigh unto him. Thou *art* / my hiding place; thou shalt preserve / me from trouble; thou shalt … compass me about with songs of / deliverance. Interlude.
I will instruct thee and teach thee / in the way which thou shalt / go: I will guide thee with mine eye. / Be ye not as the horse, … *or* as the mule, *which* have no un-derstanding: whose mouth must / be held in with bit and bridle, / lest they come near to thee. … Many sorrows *shall be* to the / wicked: but he that trus-teth in the LORD, mercy

shall com-pass him about. Be glad … in the LORD, and rejoice, ye righ-teous: and shout for joy, all / *ye that are* upright in heart.

33   Psalm 33

Rejoice in the LORD, O ye righ-teous: *for* praise is comely / for the upright. Praise the LORD with / harp: sing unto him with … the psalt'ry *and* an instrument / of ten strings. Sing unto / him a new song; play skilfully / with a loud noise. For the … word of the LORD *is* right; and all / his works *are done* in truth. / He loveth righteousness and judg-ment: the earth is full of … the goodness of the LORD. By the / word of the LORD were the / heavens made; and all the host of / them by the breath of his … mouth. He gathereth the waters of / the sea together as / an heap: he layeth up the depth / in storehouses. Let all … the earth fear the LORD: let all the / inhabitants of the / world stand in awe of him. For he / spake, and it was *done*; he … commanded, and it stood fast. The / LORD bringeth the counsel / of the heathen to nought: he ma-keth the devices of … the people of none effect. The / counsel of the LORD stand'th / for ever, the thoughts of his heart / to all generations. … Blessed *is* the nation whose God / *is* the LORD; *and* the peo-ple *whom* he hath chosen for his / own inheritance. The … LORD looketh from heaven; he be-holdeth all the sons of / men. From the place of his habi-tation he looketh on … all the inhabitants of the / earth. He fashioneth their / hearts alike; he considereth / all their works. There is no … king saved by the multitude of / an host: a mighty man / is not delivered by much strength. / An horse *is* a vain thing … for safety: neither shall he de-liver *any* by his / great strength. Behold, the eye of the / LORD *is* upon them that … fear him, upon them that hope in / his mercy; To deliv'r / their soul from death, and to keep them / alive in famine. Our … soul waiteth for the LORD: he *is* / our help and our shield. / For o'r heart shall rejoice in him, / because we have trusted … in his holy name. Let thy mer-cy, O LORD, be upon / us, according as we hope in thee.

According to the Psalm of David, when he changed his behaviour before Abimelech; who drove him away, and he departed.

I will bless the LORD at all times: / his praise *shall* ever *be* / in my mouth. My soul shall make her / boast in the LORD: *and* the … humble shall hear *thereof,* and be / glad. O magnify the / LORD with me, and let us exalt / his name together. I … sought the LORD, and he heard me, and / delivered me from all / my fears. They looked unto him, and / were lightened: their faces … were not ashamed. This poor man cried, / and the LORD heard *him,* and / saved him out of all his troubles. / The angel of the LORD … encampeth round about them that / fear him, and deliver'th / them. O taste and see that the LORD / *is* good: blessed *is* the … man *that* trusteth in him. O fear / the LORD, ye his saints: for / *there is* no want to them that fear / him. The young lions do … lack, and suffer hunger: but they / that seek the LORD shall not / want any good *thing.* Come, ye chil-dren, hearken unto me: … I will teach you the fear of the / LORD. What man *is he that* / desireth life, *and who* loveth / *many* days, that he may … see good? Keep thy tongue from evil, / and thy lips from speaking / guile. Depart from evil, do good; / seek peace, and pursue it. … The eyes of the LORD *are* upon / the righteous, and his ears / *are open* unto their cry. The / face of the LORD *is* 'gainst … them that do evil, to cut off / the remembrance of them / from the earth. *The righteous* cry, and / the LORD heareth, and *he* … delivereth them out of all / their troubles. The LORD *is* / nigh unto them that are of a / broken heart; and saveth … such as be of a contrite spi-rit. Many *are* the af-flictions of the righteous: but the / LORD delivereth him … out of them all. He keepeth all / his bones: not one of them / is broken. Evil shall slay the / wicked: and they that hate … the righteous shall be desolate. / The LORD redeemeth the / soul of his servants: and none of / them that trust in him shall … be desolate.

According to the Psalm of David.

Plead *my cause*, O LORD, with them that / strive with me: fight against / them that fight against me. Take hold / of shield and buckler, and … stand up for mine help. Draw out al-so the spear, and stop *the / way* against them that persecute / me: say unto my soul, … I *am* thy salvation. Let them / be confounded and put / to shame that seek after my soul: / let them be turned back and … brought to confusion that devise / my hurt. Let them be as / chaff before the wind: and let the / angel of the LORD chase … *them*. Let their way be dark and slip-pery: and let the an-gel of the LORD persecute them. / For without cause have they … hid for me their net *in* a pit, / *which* without cause they have / digged for my soul. O let destruc-tion come upon him at … unawares; and let his net that / he hath hid catch himself: / into that very destruction / let him fall. And my soul … shall be joyful in the LORD: it / shall rejoice in his sal-vation. All my bones shall say, LORD, / who *is* like unto thee, … which deliverest the poor from / him that is too strong for / him, yea, the poor and the needy / from him that spoileth him? … False witnesses did rise up; they / laid to my charge *things* that / I knew not. They rewarded me / evil for good *to* the … spoiling of my soul. But as for / me, when they were sick, my / clothing *was* sackcloth: I humbled / my soul with fasting; and … my prayer returned into mine / own bosom. I behaved / myself as though *he had been* my / friend *or* brother: I bowed … down heavily, as one that mour-neth *for his* mother. But / in mine adversity they re-joiced, and gathered themselves … together: *yea*, the abjects ga-thered themselves together / against me, and I knew *it* not; / they did tear *me*, and ceased … not: With hypocritical mock-ers in feasts, they gnashed u-pon me with their teeth. Lord, how long / wilt thou look on? rescue … my soul from their destructions, my / darling from the lions. / I will give thee thanks in the great / congregation: I will …praise thee *there* among much people. / Let not them that are mine / enemies wrongfully rejoice / over me: *neither* let … them wink with the eye that hate me / without a cause. For they / speak not peace: but they devise de-ceitful matters against … *them that are* quiet in the land. / Yea, they opened their mouth / wide against me, *and* said, Aha, / aha, our eye hath seen … our eye hath seen *it. This* thou hast / seen, O LORD: keep not si-lence: O Lord, be not far from me. / Stir up thyself, awake … to my judgment, *even* to my / cause, my God and my Lord. / Judge me, O LORD my God, accor-ding to thy righteousness; … and let them not rejoice over / me. Let them not say in / their hearts, Ah, so would we have it: / let them not say, We have … swallowed him up. Let them be a-shamed and brought to confu-sion together that rejoice at / mine hurt: let them be clothed … with shame and dishonour that ma-gnify *themselves* against / me. Let them shout for joy, and *let / them* be glad, that favour … my righteous cause: yea, let them say / continually, Let the / LORD be magnified, which hath plea-sure in the prosp'rity … of his servant. And my tongue shall / speak of thy righteousness / *and* of thy praise all the day long.

36   Psalm 36

To the chief Musician, *According to the Psalm* of David the servant of the LORD.

The transgression of the wicked / saith within my heart, *that / there is* no fear of God before / his eyes. For he flatt'reth … himself in his own eyes, until / his iniquity be / found to be hateful. The words of / his mouth *are* in'quity … and deceit: he hath left off to / be wise, *and* to do good. / He deviseth mischief upon / his bed; he sett'th himself … in a way *that is* not good; he / abhorreth not evil. / Thy mercy, O LORD, *is* in the / heav'ns; *and* thy faithfulness … *reacheth* unto the clouds. Thy right-eousness *is* like the great / mountains; thy judgments *are* a great / deep: O LORD, thou preserv'st … man and beast. How excellent *is* / thy lovingkindness, O / God! therefore the children of men / put their trust under the …

shadow of thy wings. They shall be / abundantly satis-fied with the fatness of thy house; / and thou shalt make them drink … of the river of thy pleasures. / For with thee *is* the foun-tain of life: in thy light shall we / see light. O continue … thy lovingkindness unto them / that know thee; and thy righ-teousness to the upright in heart. / Let not the foot of pride …come against me, and let not the / hand of the wicked re-move me. There are the workers of / iniquity fallen: … they are cast down, and shall not be / able to rise.

37   Psalm 37

According to the Psalm of David.

Fret not thyself because of e-vildoers, neither be / thou envious against the workers / of iniquity. For … they shall soon be cut down like the / grass, and wither as the / green herb. Trust in the LORD, and do / good; *so* shalt thou dwell in … the land, and verily thou shalt / be fed. Delight thyself / also in the LORD; and he shall / give thee the desires … of thine heart. Commit thy way un-to the LORD; trust also / in him; and he shall bring *it* to / pass. And he shall bring forth … thy righteousness as the light, and / thy judgment as the noon-day. Rest in the LORD, and wait pa-tiently for him: fret not … thyself because of him who pros-pereth in his way, be-cause of the man who bringeth wick-ed devices to pass. … Cease from anger, forsake wrath: fret / not thyself in any / wise to do evil. For evil-doers shall be cut off: … but those that wait upon the LORD, / they shall inherit the / earth. For yet a little while, and / the wicked *shall* not *be*: … yea, thou shalt diligently con-sider his place, and it / *shall* not *be*. But the meek shall in-herit the earth; and shall … delight themselves in the abun-dance of peace. The wicked / plotteth against the just, and gnash-eth upon him with his … teeth. The Lord shall laugh at him: for / he seeth that his day / is coming. The wicked have drawn / out the sword, and have bent … their bow, to cast down the poor and / needy, *and* to slay such / as be of upright conversa-tion. Their sword shall enter … into their own heart, and their bows / shall be broken. A littl' / that a righteous man hath *is* bet-ter than the riches of … many´ wicked. For the arms of / the wicked shall be bro-ken: but the LORD upholdeth the / righteous. The LORD knoweth … the days of the upright: and their / inheritance shall be / for ever. They shall not be a-shamed in the evil time: … and in the days of famine they / shall be satisfied. But / the wicked shall perish, and the / enemies of the LORD … *shall be* as the fat of lambs: they / shall consume; into smoke / shall they consume away. The wick-ed borroweth, and pay'th … not again: but the righteous shew-eth mercy, and giveth. / For *such as be* blessed of him / shall inherit the earth; … and *they that be* cursed of him / shall be cut off. The steps / of a *good* man are ordered by / the LORD: and he delight'th … in his way. Though he fall, he shall / not be utterly cast / down: for the LORD upholdeth *him / with* his hand. I have been … young, and *now* I am old; yet have / I not seen the righteous / forsaken, nor his seed begging / for bread. *He is* ever … merciful, and lendeth; and his / seed *is* blessed. Depart / from evil, and do good; and dwell / for evermore. For the … LORD loveth judgment, and forsa-keth not his saints; they are / preserved for ever: but the seed / of the wicked shall be … cut off. The righteous shall inhe-rit the land, and dwell there-in for ever. The mouth of the / righteous speaketh wisdom, … and his tongue talketh of judgment. / The law of his God *is* / in his heart; none of his steps shall / slide. The wicked watcheth … the righteous, and seeketh to slay / him. The LORD will not leave / him in his hand, nor condemn him / when he is judged. Wait on … the LORD, and keep his way, and he / shall exalt thee to in-herit the land: when the wicked / are cut off, thou shalt see … thou shalt see *it*. I have seen the / wicked in great power, / and spreading himself like a green / bay tree. Yet he passed 'way, … and, lo, he *was* not: yea, I sought / him, but he could not be / found. Mark the perfect *man*, and be-hold the upright: for the … end of *that* man *is* peace. But the / transgressors shall be des-troyed together: the end of the / wicked shall be cut off. … But the salvation of the righ-teous *is* of the LORD: *he / is* their strength in the time of trou-ble. And the LORD shall help … them, and deliver them: he shall / deliver them from the / wicked, and save them, because they / trust in him.

38   Psalm 38

According to the Psalm of David, to bring to remembrance.

O LORD, rebuke me not in thy / wrath: neither chasten me / in thy hot displeasure. For thine / arrows stick fast in me, … and thy hand presseth me sore. *There / is* no soundness in my / flesh because of thine anger; nei-ther *is there any* rest … in my bones because of my sin. / For mine iniquities / are gone over mine head: as an / heavy burden they are … too heavy for me. My wounds stink / *and* are corrupt because / of my foolishness. I am trou-bled; I'm bowed down greatly; … I go mourning all the day long. / For my loins are filled with / a loathsome *disease*: and *there is* / no soundness in my flesh. … I am feeble and sore broken: / I have roared by reason / of the disquietness of my / heart. Lord, all my desire … *is* before thee; and my groaning / is not hid from thee. My / heart panteth, my strength faileth me: / as for the light of mine … eyes, it also is gone from me. / My lovers and my friends / stand aloof from my sore; and my / kinsmen stand afar off. … They also that seek after my / life lay snares *for me*: and / they that seek my hurt speak mischie-vous things, and imagine … deceits all the day long. But I, / as a deaf *man*, heard not; / and *I was* as a dumb man *that* / openeth not his mouth. … Thus I was as a man that hea-reth not, and in whose mouth / *are* no reproofs. For in thee, O / LORD, do I hope: thou wilt … hear, O Lord my God. For I said, / *Hear me*, lest *otherwise* / they should rejoice over me: when / my foot slippeth, *then* they … magnify *themselves* against me. / For I *am* ready to / halt, and my sorrow *is* conti-nually before me. For … I will declare mine iniqui-ty; I will be sorry / for my sin. But mine enemies / *are* lively, *and* they are … strong: and they that hate me wrongful-ly are multiplied. *And* / they that render evil for good / are mine adversaries; … because I follow *the thing that* / good *is*. Forsake me not, / O

LORD: O my God, be not far / from me. Make haste to help … me, O Lord my salvation.

39   **Psalm 39**

To the chief Musician, *even* to Jeduthun, *According to the* Psalm of David.

I said, I will take heed to my / ways, that I sin not with / my tongue: *and* I will keep my mouth / with a bridle, while the … wicked is before me. I was / dumb with silence, I held / my peace, *even* from good; and my / sorrow was stirred. My heart … was hot within me, while I was / musing the fire burned: / *then* spake I with my tongue, LORD, make / me to know mine end, and … the measure of my days, what it / *is; that* I may know how / frail I *am*. Behold, thou hast made / my days *as* an handbreadth; … and mine age *is* as nothing be-fore thee: verily e-very man at his best state *is* al-together vanity. … Interlude.
Surely every man walketh in / a vain shew: surely they / are disquieted in vain: he / heapeth up *riches*, and … knoweth not who shall gather them. / And now, Lord, what wait I / for? my hope *is* in thee. Deli-ver me from all my trans-gressions: make me not the reproach / of the foolish. I was / dumb, I opened not my mouth; be-cause thou didst *it*. Remove … thy stroke away from me: I am / consumed by the blow of / thine hand. When thou with rebukes dost / correct man for *his sins* … for iniquity, thou makest / his beauty to consume / away like a moth: surely e-very man *is* vanity. Interlude.
Hear my prayer, O LORD, and give / ear unto my cry; hold / not thy peace at my tears: for I / *am* a stranger with thee, … *and* a sojourner, as all my / fathers *were*. O spare me, / that I may recover strength, be-fore I go hence, and be … no more.

To the chief Musician, *According to the Psalm* of David.

I waited patiently for the / LORD; and he inclined un-to me, and heard my cry. He brought / me up also out of … an horrible pit, out of the / miry clay, and set my / feet upon a rock, *and* esta-blished my goings. And he … hath put a new song in my mouth, / *even* praise unto our / God: many shall see *it*, and fear, / and shall trust in the LORD. … Bless'd *is* that man that maketh the / LORD his trust, and respec-teth not the proud, nor such as turn / aside to lies. Many, … O LORD my God, *are* thy wonder-ful works *which* thou hast done, / and thy thoughts *which are* to us-ward: / they cannot be reckoned … up in order unto thee: *if* / I would declare and speak / *of them*, they are more than can be / numbered. Sacrifice and … offering thou didst not desire; / mine ears hast thou opened: / burnt offering and sin offe-ring hast thou not requir'd. … Then said I, Lo, I come: in the / volume of the book *it* / *is* written of me, I delight / to do thy will, O my … God: yea, thy law *is* within my / heart. I have preached righteous-ness in the great congregation: / lo, I have not refrained … my lips, O LORD, thou knowest. I / have not hid thy righteous-ness within my heart; I have de-clared thy faithfulness and … thy salvation: I have not con-cealed thy lovingkindness / and thy truth from the great congre-gation. Withhold not thou … thy tender mercies from me, O / LORD: let thy lovingkind-ness and thy truth continually / preserve me. For *many* … innum'rable evils have com-passed me about: *and* mine / iniquities have taken hold / upon me, so that I … am not able to look up; they / are more than the hairs of / mine head: therefore my heart faileth / me. Be pleased, O LORD, to … deliver me: O LORD, make haste / to help me. Let them be / ashamed and confounded toge-ther that seek after my … soul to destroy it; let them be / driven backward and put / to shame that wish me evil. Let / them be desolate for … a reward of their shame that say / unto me, Aha, a-ha. Let all those that seek thee re-joice and be glad in thee: … let such as love thy salvation / say continually, The / LORD be magnified. But I *am* / poor and needy; *yet* the … Lord thinketh upon me: thou *art* / my help and my deli-verer; make no tarrying, O / my God.

41   Psalm 41

To the chief Musician, *According to the* Psalm of David.

Blessed *is* he that conside-reth the poor: the LORD will / deliver him in time of trou-ble. The LORD will preserve … him, and keep him alive; *and* he / shall be blessed upon / the earth: and thou wilt not deli-ver him unto the will … of his enemies. *And* the LORD / will strengthen him upon / the bed of languishing: thou wilt / make all his bed in his … sickness. I said, LORD, be merci-ful unto me: heal my / soul; for I have sinned against thee. / Mine enemies speak ev'l … of me, When shall he die, and his / name perish? And if he / come to see *me*, he speaketh va-nity: his heart gath'reth … iniquity to itself; *when* / he goeth abroad, he / telleth *it*. All that hate me whis-per together against … me: against me do they devise / my hurt. An evil di-sease, *say they*, cleaveth fast unto / him: *now* that he lieth … he shall rise up no more. Yea, mine / own familiar friend, in / whom I trusted, which did eat of / my bread, hath lifted up … *his* heel against me. But thou, O / LORD, be merciful un-to me, and raise me up, that I / may requite them. By this … I know that thou favourest me, / because mine enemy / doth not triumph over me. And / as for me, thou uphold'st … me in mine integrity, and / settest me before thy / face for ever. Blessed *be* the / LORD God of Israel … from everlasting, and to e-verlasting. Amen, and A-men.

42   Psalm 42

To the chief Musician, Maschil, for the sons of Korah.

As the hart panteth after the / water brooks, so panteth / my soul after thee, O God. My / soul thirsteth for God, for … the living God: when shall I come / and appear before God? / My tears have been my meat day and / night, while they always say … unto me, Where *is* thy God? When / I remember these *things*, / I pour out my soul in me: for / I had gone with *them, there … with* the multitude, I went with / them to the house of God, / with the voice of joy and praise, with / a multitude that kept … holyday. Why art thou cast down, / O my soul? and *why* art / thou disquieted in me? hope / thou in God: for I shall … yet praise him *for* the help of his / count'nance. O my God, my / soul is cast down within me: there-fore will I remember … thee from the land of Jordan, and / of the Hermonites, from / the hill Mizar. Deep calleth un-to deep at the noise of … thy waterspouts: all thy waves and / thy billows are gone o-ver me. *Yet* the LORD will command / his lovingkindness in … the daytime, and in the night his / song *shall be* with me, *and* / my prayer unto the God of / my life. I will say to … God my rock, Why hast thou forgot-ten me? why go I mour-ning because of the oppression / of the enemy? *As* … with a sword in my bones, mine e-nemies reproach me; while / they say daily unto me, Where / *is* thy God? Why art thou … cast down, O my soul? and why art / thou disquieted with-in me? hope thou in God: for I / shall yet praise him, *who is* … the health of my countenance, and / my God.

43   Psalm 43

Judge me, O God, and plead my cause / against an ungodly / nation: O deliver me from / the deceitful, unjust … man. For thou *art* the God of my / strength: why dost thou cast me / off? why go I mourning because / of the oppression of … the enemy? O send out thy / light and thy truth: let them / lead me; let them bring me unto /

thy holy hill, and to … thy tabernacles. Then will I / go unto the altar / of God, unto God my excee-ding joy: yea, upon the … harp will I praise thee, O God my / God. Why art thou cast down, / O my soul? and why art thou dis-quieted within me? … hope in God: for I shall yet praise / him, *who is* the health of / my countenance, and my God.

44   Psalm 44

To the chief Musician for the sons of Korah, Maschil.

We have heard with our ears, O God, / our fathers have told us, / *what* work thou didst in their days, in / the times of old. *How* thou … didst drive out the heathen with thy / hand, and plantedst them; *how* / thou didst afflict the people, and / cast them out. For they got … not the land in possession by / their own sword, neither did / their own arm save them: but thy right / hand, and thine arm, and the … light of thy countenance, because / thou hadst a favour un-to them. Thou art my King, O God: / command deliv'rances … for Jacob. Through thee will we push / down o'r enemies: through / thy name will we tread them under / that rise up against us. … For I will not trust in my bow, / neither shall my sword save / me. But thou hast saved us from ou-r enemies, and hast … put them to shame that hated us. / In God we boast all the / day long, and praise thy name for ever. Interlude.

But thou hast cast off, and put us / to shame; and goest not / forth with our armies. Thou makest / us to turn back from the … enemy: and they which hate us / spoil for themselves. Thou hast / given us like sheep *appointed* / for meat; and hast scattered … us among the heathen. Thou sel-lest thy people for nought, / and dost not increase *thy wealth* by / their price. Thou makest us … a reproach to our neighbours, a / scorn and a derision / to them that are round about us. / Thou mak'st us a byword … among the heathen, a shaking / of the head among the / people. My confusion *is* con-tinu'lly before me, … and the shame of my face hath co-vered me, For the voice of

/ him that reproacheth and blasphe-meth; by reason of the … enemy and avenger. All / this is come on us; yet / have we not forgotten thee, nei-ther have we dealt falsely … in thy covenant. Our heart / is not turned back *from thee,* / neither have our steps declined / from thy way; Though thou hast … sore broken us in the place of / dragons, and covered us / with the shadow of death. If we / have forgotten the name … of our God, or stretched out our / hands to a strange god; Shall / not God search this out? for he know-eth the secrets of the … heart. Yea, for thy sake are we killed / all the day long; we are / counted as sheep for the slaughter. / Awake, why sleepest thou, … O Lord? arise, cast *us* not off / for ever. Wherefore hi-dest thou thy face, *and* forgettest / our affliction and our … oppression? For our soul is bowed / down to the dust: our / belly cleaveth unto the earth. / Arise for our help, … and redeem us for thy mercies' / sake.

45   **Psalm 45**

To the chief Musician upon Shoshannim, for the sons of Korah, Maschil, A Song of loves.

My heart is inditing a good / matter: I speak of the / things which I have made touching the / king: my tongue *is* the pen … of a ready writer. Thou art / fairer than the children / of men: grace is poured into thy / lips: therefore God hath bless'd … thee for ever. Gird thy sword u-pon *thy* thigh, O *most* migh-ty, with thy glory and *with* thy / majesty. And in thy … majesty ride prosperously / because of truth and meek-ness *and* righteousness; thy right hand / shall teach thee terrible … things. Thine arrows *are* sharp in the / heart of the king's ene-mies; *whereby* the people fall un-der thee. Thy throne, O God, … *is* for ever and ever: the / sceptre of thy kingdom / *is* a right sceptre. Thou lovest / righteousness, and hatest … wickedness: therefore God, thy God, / hath anointed thee with / the oil of gladness above thy / fellows. All thy garments … *smell* of myrrh, and aloes, *and* / cassia, out of the / ivory palaces, whereby / they

have made thee glad. Kings' … daughters *were* among thy honou-
rable women: upon / thy right hand did stand the queen in / gold of
Ophir. Hearken, … O daughter, and consider, and / incline thine ear;
forget / also thine own people, and thy / father's house; So shall the
… king greatly desire thy beau-ty: for he *is* thy Lord; / and worship
thou him. And the daugh-ter of Tyre *shall be … there* with a gift;
even the rich / among the people shall / intreat thy favour. The
king's daugh-ter *is* all glorious … within: her clothing *is* of
wrought / gold. She shall be brought un-to the king in raiment of
nee-dlework: the virgins her … companions that follow her shall /
be brought unto thee. With / gladness and rejoicing shall they / be
brought: they shall enter … into the king's palace. Instead / of thy
fathers shall be / thy children, whom thou mayest make / princes in
all the earth. … I will make thy name to be re-membered in all
gene-rations: therefore shall the people / praise thee for ev'r and
ev'r.

46   Psalm 46

To the chief Musician for the sons of Korah, A Song upon Alamoth.

God *is* our refuge and strength, a / very present help in / trouble.
Therefore will not we fear, / though the earth be removed, … and
though the mountains be carried / into the midst of the / sea; *Though*
the waters thereof roar / *and* be troubled, *though* the … mountains
shake with the swelling there-of. Interlude.
There is a river, the streams where-of shall make glad the ci-ty of
God, the holy *place* of / the tabernacles of … the most High. God *is*
in the midst / of her; she shall not be / moved: God shall help her,
and that right / early. The heathen raged, … the kingdoms were
moved: he uttered / his voice, the earth melted. / The LORD of hosts
is with us; the / God of Jacob *is* our … refuge. Interlude.
Come, behold the works of the LORD, / what desolations he / hath
made in the earth. He maketh / wars to cease unto the … end of the
earth; he breaketh the / bow, and cutteth the spear / in sunder; he

burneth the cha-riot in the fire. … Be still, and know that I *am* God: / I will be exalted / among the heathen, I will be / exalted in the earth. … The LORD of hosts *is* with us; the / God of Jacob *is* our / refuge. Interlude.

47   Psalm 47

To the chief Musician, *According to the* Psalm for the sons of Korah.

O clap your hands, all ye people; / shout unto God with the / voice of triumph. For the LORD most / high *is* terrible; *he* … *is* a great King over all the / earth. He shall subdue the / people under us, and the na-tions under our feet. … He shall choose our inheri-tance for us, the excel-lency of Jacob whom he loved. Interlude.
God is gone up with a shout, the / LORD with the sound of a / trumpet. Sing praises to God, sing / praises: sing praises to … our King, sing praises. For God / *is* the King of all the / earth: sing ye praises with under-standing. God reign'th over … the heathen: God sitteth upon / the throne of his holi-ness. The princes of the people / are gathered together, … *even* the people of the God / of Abraham: for the / shields of the earth *belong* to God: / he is greatly exalt'd.

48   Psalm 48

According to the Song *and* Psalm for the sons of Korah.

Great *is* the LORD, and greatly to / be praised in the city / of our God, *there in* the moun-tain of his holiness. … Beautiful for situation, / the joy of the whole earth, / *is* mount Zion, *on* the sides of / the north, the city of … the great King. God is known *there* in / her palaces for a / refuge. For, lo, the kings were as-sembled, *and* they passed by … together. They saw *it, and* so / they marvelled; *and* they were / troubled, *and* hasted away. Fear / took hold upon

them there, ... *and* pain, as of a woman in tra-vail. Thou breakest
the ships / of Tarshish with an east wind. As / we have heard, so
have we ... seen in the city of the LORD / of hosts, in the city / of
our God: God will esta-blish it for evermore. Interlude.
We have thought of thy lovingkind-ness, O God, in the midst / of
thy temple. According to / thy name, O God, so *is* ... thy praise unto
the ends of the / earth: thy right hand is full / of righteousness. Let
mount Zion / rejoice, let the daughters ... of Judah be glad, because
of / thy judgments. Walk about / Zion, and go round about her: / tell
the towers thereof. ... Mark ye well her bulwarks, consi-der her
palaces; that / ye may tell *it* to the gene-ration following. For ... this
God *is* our God for e-ver and ever: he will / be our guide *even* unto /
death.

49 Psalm 49

To the chief Musician, *According to the* Psalm for the sons of
Korah.

Hear this, all *ye* people; give ear, / all *ye* inhabitants / of the world:
Both low and high, rich / and poor, together. My ... mouth shall
speak of wisdom; and the / meditation of my / heart *shall be* of
understanding. / I will incline mine ear ... to a parable: I will o-pen
my dark saying on / the harp. Wherefore should I fear in / the days
of evil, *when* ... the iniquity of my heels / shall compass me about? /
They that trust in their wealth, and boast / themselves in their riches
... in the multitude of their rich-es; None *of them* can by / any
means redeem his brother, / nor give to God ransom ... a ransom for
him: (For the re-demption of their soul *is* / precious, and it ceaseth
for e-ver:) That he should still live ... for ever, *and* not see corruption. For he seeth *that* / wise men die, likewise the fool, the / brutish
person perish, ... and leave their wealth to others. Their / inward
thought *is, that* their / houses *shall continue* for e-ver, their dwelling
places ... to all generations; they call / *their* lands after their own /
names. Nevertheless man *being* / in honour abideth ... not: he is like

the beasts *that* pe-rish. This their way *is* their / folly: yet their posterity / *they* approve their sayings. Interlude.

Like sheep they are laid in the grave; / death shall feed on them; and / the upright shall have dominion / over them in t'morning; ... and their beauty shall consume in / the grave from their dwelling. / But God will redeem my soul from / the power of the grave: ... for he shall receive me. Interlude.

Be not thou afraid when one is / made rich, *and* when the glo-ry of his house is increased; For / when he dieth he shall ... carry nothing away: his glo-ry shall not descend af-ter him. Though while he lived he blessed / his soul: and *men* will praise ... thee, when thou doest well to thy-self. He shall go to the / generation of his fathers; / they shall never see light. ... Man *that is* in honour, and un-derstandeth not, is like / the beasts *that* perish.

50   Psalm 50

According to the Psalm of Asaph.

The mighty God, *even* the LORD, / hath spoken, and called the / earth from the rising of the sun / unto the going down ... thereof. Out of Zion, the per-fection of beauty, God / hath shined. Our God shall come, and shall / not keep silence: a fire ... shall devour before him, and / it shall be very tem-pestuous round about him. He shall / call to the heavens from ... above, and *call* to the earth, that / he may judge his people. / Gather my saints together to / me; those *people* that have ... made a covenant with me by / sacrifice. And the hea-vens shall declare his righteousness: / for God *is* judge himself. Interlude.

Hear, O my people, and I will / speak; O Israel, and / I will testify against thee: / I *am* God, *even* thy ... God. I will not reprove thee for / thy sacrifices or / thy burnt offerings, *to have been* / continually before ... me. I will take no bullock out / of thy house, *nor* he goats / out of thy folds. For every beast / of the forest *is* mine, ... *and* the cattle upon a thou-sand hills. I know all the / fowls of the mountains: and the wild / beasts of the field *are* mine. … If I were hungry, I would not / tell thee: for the world *is* / mine, and the fulness thereof. Will / I eat the flesh of bulls, … or drink the blood of goats? Offer / unto God thanksgiving; / and pay thy vows unto the most / High: And call upon me … in the day of trouble: I will / deliver thee, and thou / shalt glorify me. But unto / the wicked God saith, What … hast thou to do to declare my / statutes, or *that* thou should'st / take my covenant in thy mouth? / Seeing *that* thou hatest … instruction, and castest my words / behind thee. When thou saw'st / a thief, then thou consentedst with him, / hast been partaker … with adulterers. Thou givest / thy mouth to evil, and / thy tongue frameth deceit. Thou sit-test *and* speakest against … thy brother; thou slanderest thine / own mother's son. These *things* / hast thou done, and I kept silence; / thou thoughtest that I was … altogether *such an one* as / thyself: *but* I will re-prove thee, and set *them* in order / before thine eyes. *And* now … consider this, ye that forget / God, lest I tear *you* in / pieces, and *there be* none to de-liver. Whoso off'reth … praise glorifieth me: and to / him that ord'reth *his* con-versation *aright* will I shew / the salvation of God.

51   Psalm 51

To the chief Musician, *According to the* Psalm of David, when Nathan the prophet came unto him, after he had gone in to Bath-sheba.

Have mercy upon me, O God, / according to thy lo-vingkindness: according unto / the multitude of thy … tender mercies blot out my trans-gressions. Wash me throughly / from mine iniquity, and cleanse / me from my sin. For I … acknowledge my transgressions: and / my sin *is* ever be-fore me. Against thee, thee only, / have I sinned, and done *this* … evil in thy sight: that thou migh-test be justified when / thou speakest, *and* be clear when thou / judgest. Behold, I was … shapen in iniquity; and / in sin did my mother / conceive me. Behold, thou desi-rest truth in the inward … parts: and in the hidden *part* thou / shalt make me to know wis-dom. Purge me with hyssop, and I / shall be clean: wash me, and … I shall be whiter than snow. Make / me to hear joy and glad-ness; *that* the bones *which* thou hast bro-ken may rejoice. Hide thy … face from my sins, and blot out all / mine iniquities. Cre-ate in me a clean heart, O God; / renew a right spirit … within me. Cast me not away / from thy presence; and take / not thy holy spirit from me. / Restore unto me the … joy of thy salvation; and up-hold me *with thy* free spi-rit. *Then* will I teach transgressors / thy ways; and sinners shall … be converted unto thee. De-liver me from bloodguil-tiness, O God, thou God of my / salvation: *and* my tongue … shall sing aloud of thy righteous-ness. O Lord, open thou / my lips; and my mouth shall shew forth / thy praise. For thou desir'st … not sacrifice; else would I give / *it*: thou delightest not / in burnt offering. The sacri-fices of God *are* a … broken spirit: a broken and / a contrite heart, O God, / thou wilt not despise. Do good in / thy good pleasure unto … Zion: build thou the walls of Je-rusalem. Then shalt thou / be pleased with the sacrifices / of righteousness, with burnt … offering and whole burnt offe-ring: then shall they offer / bullocks upon thine altar.

52   **Psalm 52**

To the chief Musician, Maschil, *According to the Psalm* of David, when Doeg the Edomite came and told Saul, and said unto him, David is come to the house of Ahimelech.

Why boastest thou thyself in mis-chief, O mighty man? *while* / the goodness of God *endureth* / continually. Thy tongue … deviseth mischiefs; like a sharp / rasor, working deceit-fully. Thou lov'st evil more than / good; *and* lying rather … than to speak righteousness. Interlude.
Thou lovest all devouring words, / O *thou* deceitful tongue. / God shall likewise destroy thee for / ever, he shall take thee … away, and

pluck thee out of *thy* / dwelling place, and root thee / out of the land of the living. Interlude.

The righteous also shall see, and / fear, and shall laugh at him: / Lo, *this is* the man *that* made not / God his strength; but trusted … in the abundance of his rich-es, *and* strengthened himself / in his wickedness. But I *am* / like a green olive tree … in the house of God: I trust in / the mercy of God for / ever and ever. I will praise / thee for ever, because … thou hast done *it*: and I will wait / on thy name; for *it is* / good before thy saints.

53   **Psalm 53**

To the chief Musician upon Mahalath, Maschil, *According to the Psalm* of David.

The fool hath said in his heart, *There / is* no God. Corrupt are / they, and have done abomina-ble iniquity: *there … is* none that doeth good. God looked / down from heaven upon / the children of men, to see if / there were *any* that did … understand, that did seek God. E-very one of them is gone / back: they are altogether be-come filthy; *there is* none … that doeth good, no, not one. Have / the workers of ini-quity no knowledge? who eat up / my people *as* they eat … bread: they have not called upon God. / There were they in great fear, / *where* no fear was: for God hath scat-tered the bones of him that … encampeth *against* thee: thou hast / put *them* to shame, because / God hath despised them. Oh that the / salvation of Isr'el … *were come* out of Zion! When God / bringeth back the capti-vity of his people, Jacob / shall rejoice, *and* Isr'el … shall be glad.

To the chief Musician on Neginoth, Maschil, *According to the Psalm* of David, when the Ziphims came and said to Saul, Doth not David hide himself with us?

Save me, O God, by thy name, and / judge me by thy strength. Hear / my prayer, O God; *and* give ear / to the words of my mouth. … For strangers are risen up a-gainst me, and oppressors / *they* seek after my soul: they have / not set God before them. Interlude.
Behold, God *is* mine helper: the / Lord *is* with them that up-hold my soul. He shall reward e-vil unto mine en'mies: … cut them off in thy truth. I will / freely sacrifice un-to thee: I will praise thy name, O / LORD; for *it is* good. For … he hath delivered me out of / all trouble: and mine eye / hath seen *his desire* upon / mine enemies.

To the chief Musician on Neginoth, Maschil, *According to the Psalm* of David.

Give ear to my prayer, O God; / and hide not thyself from / my supplication. Attend un-to me, and hear me: I … mourn in my complaint, and make a / noise; Because of the voice / of the enemy, because of / the oppression of the … wicked: for they cast iniqui-ty upon me, and in / wrath they hate me. My heart is sore / pained within me: and the … terrors of death are fallen u-pon me. Fearfulness and / trembling are come upon me, and / horror hath ov'rwhelmed me. … And I said, Oh that I had wings / like a dove! *for then* would / I fly away, and be at rest. / Lo, *then* would I wander … far off, *and* remain in the wil-derness. Interlude.
I would hasten my escape from / the windy storm *and the* / tempest. Destroy, O Lord, *and* di-vide their tongues: for I have … seen violence and strife in the / city. Day and night they / go about it upon the walls / thereof: mischief also … and sorrow *are* in the

midst of / it. Wickedness *is* in / the midst thereof: deceit and guile / depart not from her streets. ... For *it was* not an enemy / *that* reproached me; then I / could have borne *it*: neither *was it* / he that hated me *that* ... did magnify *himself* against / me; then I would have hid / myself from him: But *it was* thou, / a man mine equal, my ... guide, and mine acquaintance. We took / sweet counsel together, / *and* walked unto the house of God / in company. Let death ... seize upon them, *and* let them go / down quick into hell: for / wickedness *is* in their dwellings, / among them. As for me, ... I will call upon God; and the / LORD shall save me. Ev'ning, / and morning, and at noon, will I / pray, and cry aloud: and ... he shall hear my voice. He hath de-livered my soul in peace / from the battle *that was* against / me: for there were many ... with me. God shall hear, and afflict / them, even he that a-bideth of old. Interlude.
Because they have no changes, there-fore they fear not God. He / hath put forth his hands against such / as be at peace with him: ... he hath broken his covenant. / *The words* of his mouth were / smoother than butter, but war *was* / in his heart: his words were ... softer than oil, yet *were* they drawn / swords. Cast thy burden on / the LORD, and he shall sustain thee: / he shall never suffer ... the righteous to be moved. But thou, / O God, shalt bring them down / into the pit of destruction: / bloody and deceitful ... men shall not live out half their days; / but I will trust in thee.

56   **Psalm 56**

To the chief Musician upon Jonath-elem-rechokim, *According to the* Michtam of David, when the Philistines took him in Gath.

Be merciful unto me, O / God: for man would swallow / me up; he fighting daily op-presseth me. Mine en'mies ... would daily swallow *me* up: for / *they be* many that fight / against me, O thou most High. What / time I am afraid, I ... will trust in thee. In God I will / praise his word, in God I / have put my trust; I will not fear / what flesh can do to me. ... Every day they wrest my words: all /

their thoughts *are* against me / for evil. They gather themselves / together, *and* they hide … themselves, they mark my steps, when they / wait for my soul. Shall they / escape by iniquity? in / *thine* anger cast down the … people, O God. Thou tellest my / wanderings: put thou my / tears into thy bottle: *are they* / not in thy book? When I … cry *unto thee*, then shall mine e-nemies turn back: this I / know; for God *is* for me. In God / will I praise *his* word: in … the LORD will I praise *his* word. In / God have I put my trust: / I will not be afraid what man / can do unto me. Thy … vows *are* upon me, O God: I / will render praises to / thee. For thou hast delivered my / soul from death: *wilt* not *thou* … *deliver* my feet from falling, / that I may walk before / God in the light of the living?

57   Psalm 57

To the chief Musician, Al-taschith, *According to the* Michtam of David, when he fled from Saul in the cave.

Be merciful unto me, O / God, be merciful to / me: for my soul trusteth in thee: / yea, in the shadow of … thy wings will I make my refuge, / 'til *these* calamities / be overpast. I will cry un-to God most high; to God … that performeth *all things* for me. / He shall send from heav'n, and / save me *from* the reproach of him / that would swallow me up. Interlude.
God shall send forth his mercy and / his truth. My soul *is* 'mong / lions: *and* I lie *even a-mong* them that are set on … fire, *even* the sons of men, / whose teeth *are* spears and *are* / arrows, and their tongue a sharp sword. / Be thou exalted, O … God, above the heavens; *let* thy / glory *be* above all / the earth. They have prepared a net / for my steps; my soul is … bowed down: they have digged a pit be-fore me, into the midst / whereof they are fallen *themselves*. Interlude.
My heart is fixed, O God, my heart / is fixed: I will sing and / give praise. Awake up, my glory; / awake, psalt'ry and harp: … I *myself* will awake early. / I will praise thee, O Lord, / among the people: I

will sing / unto thee among the … nations. For thy mercy *is* great / unto the heavens, and / thy truth unto the clouds. Be thou / exalted, O God, 'bove … the heavens: *let* thy glory *be* / above all the earth.

58   **Psalm 58**

To the chief Musician, Al-taschith, *According to the* Michtam of David.

Do ye indeed speak righteousness, / O congregation? do / ye judge uprightly, O ye sons / of men? Yea, in heart ye … work wickedness; ye weigh the vi-olence of your hands in / the earth. The wicked are estranged / from the womb: they go 'stray … as soon as they be born, speaking / lies. Their poison *is* like / the poison of a serpent: *they / are* like the deaf adder … *that* stoppeth her ear; Which will not / hearken to the voice of / charmers, charming never so wise-ly. Break their teeth, O God, … in their mouth: break out the great teeth / of the young lions, O / LORD. Let them melt 'way as waters / *which* run continually: … *when* he bendeth *his bow to shoot* / his arrows, let them be / as cut in pieces. As a snail / *which* melteth, let *every* … *one of them* pass away: *like* the / untimely birth of a / woman, *that* they may not see the / sun. Before your pots can … feel the thorns, he shall take them a-way as with a whirlwind, / both living, and in *his* wrath. The / righteous shall rejoice when … he seeth the vengeance: he shall / wash his feet in the blood / of the wicked. So that a man / shall say, Verily *there* … *is* a reward for the righteous: / verily he is a / God that judgeth in the earth.

To the chief Musician, Al-taschith, *According to the* Michtam of David; when Saul sent, and they watched the house to kill him.

Deliver me from mine ene-mies, O my God: defend / me from them that rise up against / me. Deliver me from … the workers of iniquity, / and save me from bloody / men. For, lo, they lie in wait for / my soul: the mighty are … gathered against me; not *for* my / transgression, nor *for* my / sin, O LORD. They run and prepare / themselves without *my* fault: … awake to help me, and behold. / Thou therefore, O LORD God / of hosts, the God of Israel, / awake to visit all … the heathen: be not merciful / to any wicked trans-gressors. Interlude.
They return at evening: they / make a noise like a dog, / and go round about the city. / Behold, they belch out with … their mouth: swords *are* in their lips: for / who, *say they*, doth hear? But / thou, O LORD, shalt laugh at them; thou / shalt have all the heathen … in derision. *Because of* his / strength will I wait upon / thee: for God *is* my defence. The / God of my mercy shall … prevent me: God shall let me see / *my desire* upon / mine enemies. Slay them not, lest / my people forget: *but* … scatter them by thy power; and / bring them down, O Lord our / shield. *For* the sin of their mouth *and* / the words of their lips let … them even be taken in their / pride: and for cursing and / lying *which* they speak. Consume *them* / in wrath, consume *them*, that … they *may* not *be*: let them know that / God ruleth in Jacob / unto the ends of the earth. Interlude.
And at ev'ning let them return; / let them make a noise like / a dog, and go round about the / city. Let them wander … up and down for meat, and grudge if / they be not satisfied. / But I will sing of thy power; / yea, I will sing aloud … I'll sing of thy mercy in the / morning: for thou hast been / my defence and refuge in the / day of my trouble. To … thee, O my strength, will I sing: for / God *is* my defence, *and* / the God of my mercy.

To the chief Musician upon Shushan-eduth, *According to the* Michtam of David, to teach; when he strove with Aram-naharaim and with Aram-zobah, when Joab returned, and smote of Edom in the valley of salt twelve thousand.

O God, thou hast cast us off, thou / hast scattered us, thou hast / been displeased; O turn thyself to / us again. Thou hast made … the earth to tremble; thou hast bro-ken it: heal the breaches / thereof; for it shaketh. Thou hast / shewed thy people hard things: … thou hast made us to drink the wine / of astonishment. Thou / hast given a banner to them / that fear thee, that it may … be displayed because of the truth. Interlude.
That thy beloved may be de-livered; save *with* thy right / hand, and hear me. God hath spoken / in his holiness; I … will rejoice, I will divide She-chem, and *will* mete out the / valley of Succoth. Gilead / *is* mine, and Manasseh … *is* mine; Ephraim also *is* / the strength of mine head; *and* / Judah *is* my lawgiver; Mo-ab *is* my washpot; *and* … over Edom will I cast out / my shoe: Philistia, / triumph thou because of me. Who / will bring me *into* the … strong city? who will lead me in-to Edom? *Wilt* not thou, / O God, *which* hadst cast us off? and / *thou*, O God, *which* didst not … go out with our armies? Give / us help from trouble: for / vain *is* the help of man. Through God / we shall do valiantly: … for he *it is that* shall tread down / our enemies.

To the chief Musician upon Neginah, *According to the Psalm* of David.

Hear my cry, O God; attend un-to my prayer. From the / end of the earth will I cry un-to thee, when my heart is … overwhelmed: lead me to the rock / *that* is higher than I. / For thou hast been a shelter for / me, *and* a strong tower … from the enemy. I will a-bide in thy tab'nacle / for ever: *and* I will trust in / the covert of thy wings. Interlude.

For thou, O God, hast heard my vows: / thou hast given *me* the / heritage of those that fear thy / name. Thou wilt prolong the … king's life: *and* his years as many / generations. He shall / abide before God for ever: / O prepare mercy and … truth, *which* may preserve him. So will / I sing praise unto thy / name for ever, that I may dai-ly perform my vows.

62   **Psalm 62**

To the chief Musician, to Jeduthun, *According to the* Psalm of David.

Truly my soul waiteth upon / God: from him *cometh* my / salvation. He only *is* my / rock and my salvation; … *he is* my defence; I shall not / be greatly moved. How long / will ye imagine mischief a-gainst a man? ye shall be … slain all of you: as a bowing / wall *shall ye be, and as* / a tottering fence. They only / consult to cast *him* down … from his excellency: they de-light in lies: they bless with / their mouth, but they curse inwardly. Interlude.

My soul, wait thou only upon / God; for my expecta-tion *is* from him. He only *is* / my rock, my salvation: … *he is* my defence; I shall not / be moved. In God *is* my / salvation and my glory: the / rock of my strength, *and* my … refuge, *is* in God. Trust in him / at all times; ye people, / pour out your heart before him: God / *is* a refuge for us. Interlude.

Surely men of low degree *are* / vanity, *and* men of / high degree *are* a lie: to be / laid in the balance, they … *are* altogether *lighter* than / vanity. Trust not in / oppression, and become not vain / in robbery: if rich's … increase, set not your heart *upon* / *them*. God hath spoken once; / twice have I heard this; that power / *belongeth* unto

God. … Also unto thee, O Lord, *be-longeth* mercy: for thou / renderest to every man a-ccording to his work.

63   Psalm 63

According to the Psalm of David, when he was in the wilderness of Judah.

O God, thou *art* my God; early / will I seek thee: my soul / thirsteth for thee, my flesh longeth / for thee in a dry and … thirsty land, where no water is; / To see thy power and / thy glory, so *as* I have seen / thee in the sanctuary. … Because thy lovingkindness *is* / better than life, my lips / shall praise thee. Thus will I bless thee / while I live: I will lift … up my hands in thy name. My soul / shall be satisfied as / *with* marrow and fatness; my mouth / shall praise *thee* with joyful … lips: When I remember thee u-pon my bed, *and* medi-tate on thee in the *night* watches. / Because thou hast been my … help, therefore in the shadow of / thy wings will I rejoice. / My soul followeth hard after / thee: thy right hand uphold'th … me. But those *that* seek my soul, to / destroy *it*, shall go in-to the lower parts of the earth. / They shall fall by the sword: … they shall be a portion for fox-es. But the king shall re-joice in God; every one that swea-reth by him shall glory: … but the mouth of them that speak lies / shall be stopped.

64   Psalm 64

To the chief Musician, *According to the* Psalm of David.

Hear my voice, O God, in my pray'r: / preserve my life from fear / of the enemy. Hide me from / the secret counsel of … the wicked; from the insurrec-tion of the workers of / iniquity: Who whet their tongue / like a sword, *and* bend *their* … *bows to shoot* their arrows, *even* / bitter words: That they may / shoot in secret at the perfect: /

suddenly do they shoot … at him, and fear not. They encou-rage themselves *in* an e-vil matter: they commune of lay-ing snares privily; they … say, Who shall see them? They search out / iniquities; *and* they / accomplish a diligent search: / both the inward *thought* of … every one *of them*, and the heart, / *is* deep. But God shall shoot / at them *with* an arrow; sudden-ly shall they be wounded. … So they shall make their own tongue to / fall upon themselves: all / that see them shall flee away. And / all men shall fear, and shall … declare the work of God; for they / shall wisely consider / of his doing. The righteous shall / be glad in the LORD, and … shall trust in him; and all the up-right in heart shall glory.

65   Psalm 65

To the chief Musician, *According to the* Psalm *and* Song of David.

Praise waiteth for thee, O God, in / Sion: and unto thee / shall the vow be performed. O thou / that hearest prayer, to … thee shall all flesh come. Iniqui-ties prevail against me: / *as for* our transgressions, thou shalt / purge them away. Blessed … *is the man whom* thou choosest, and / causest to approach *un-to thee, that* he may dwell in thy / courts: we shall be sat'sfied … with the goodness of thy house, *e-ven* of thy holy tem-ple. *By* terrible things in right-eousness wilt thou answer … us, O God of o'r salvation; / *who art* the confidence / of all the ends of the earth, and / of them that are afar … off *upon* the sea: Which by his / strength setteth fast the moun-tains; *being* girded with power: / Which stilleth the noise of … the seas, *and* the noise of their waves, / and the tumult of the / people. They also that dwell in / the uttermost parts are … afraid at thy tokens: thou ma-kest the outgoings of / the morning and evening to / rejoice. Thou visitest … the earth, and waterest it: thou / greatly enrichest it / with the river of God, *which* is / full of water: *and* thou … preparest them corn, when thou hast / so provided for it. / Thou waterest the ridges there-of abundantly: thou … settlest the furrows thereof: thou / makest it soft with show'rs: / thou blessest the springing thereof. / Thou crownest the year with … thy goodness; and thy paths drop fat-ness. They drop *upon* the / pastures of the wilderness: and / the little hills rejoice … on every side. The pastures are / clothed with flocks; the valleys / also are covered over with / corn; they shout for joy, they … also sing.

66   Psalm 66

To the chief Musician, *According to the* Song *or* Psalm *66.*

Make a joyful noise unto God, / all ye lands: Sing forth the / honour of his name: make his praise / glorious. Say unto … God, How terrible *art thou in* / thy works! through the greatness / of thy power shall thine ene-mies submit themselves to … thee. All the earth shall worship thee, / and shall sing unto thee; / they shall sing *to* thy name. Interlude.
Come and see the works of God: *he / is* terrible *in his* / doing toward the children of / men. He turned the sea to … dry *land*: they went through the flood on / foot: there did we rejoice / in him. He ruleth by his po-wer for ever; his eyes … behold the nations: let not the / rebellious exalt them-selves. Interlude.
O bless our God, ye people, and / make the voice of his praise / to be heard: Which holdeth our soul / in life, and suffereth … not our feet to be moved. For / thou, O God, hast proved us: / thou hast tried us, as silver is / tried. Thou brought'st us into … the net; thou laidst affliction u-pon our loins. Thou hast / caused men to ride over our / heads; we went through fire … and through water: but thou broughtest / us out into a weal-thy *place.* I will go into thy / house with burnt offerings: … I will pay thee my vows, Which my / lips have uttered, and my / mouth hath spoken, when I was in / trouble. I will offer … I'll offer unto thee burnt sa-crifices of fatlings, / with the incense of rams; I will / offer bullocks with goats. Interlude.
Come *and* hear, all ye that fear God, / and I will declare what / he hath done for my soul. I cried / unto him with my mouth, … and he was extolled with my tongue. / If I regard ini-quity in my heart, the

Lord will / not hear *me*: *But* ver'ly ... God hath heard *me*; he hath atten-ded to the voice of my / prayer. Blessed *be* God, which hath / not turned away my pray'r, ... nor his mercy from me.

67   Psalm 67

To the chief Musician on Neginoth, *According to the* Psalm *or* Song *67*.

God be merciful unto us, / and bless us; *and* cause his / face to shine upon us; Interlude.
That thy way may be known upon / earth, thy saving health a-mong all nations. Let the people / praise thee, O God; let all ... the people praise thee. O let the / nations be glad and sing / for joy: for thou shalt judge the peo-ple righteously, and *thou ... shalt* govern the nations upon / earth. Interlude.
Let the people praise thee, O God; / let all the people praise / thee. *Then* shall the earth yield her in-crease; *and* God, *even* our ... own God, shall bless us. God shall bless / us; and all the ends of / the earth shall fear him.

68   Psalm 68

To the chief Musician, *According to the* Psalm *or* Song of David.

Let God arise, let his ene-mies be scattered: let them / also that hate him flee before / him. As smoke is driven ... away, *so* drive *them* away: as / wax melteth before the / fire, *so* let the wicked pe-rish at the presence of ... God. But let the righteous be glad; / let them rejoice before / God: yea, let them exceedingly / rejoice. Sing unto God, ... sing praises to his name: extol / him that rideth upon / the heavens by his name JAH, and / rejoice before him. A ... father of the fatherless, and / a judge of the widows, / *is* God in his holy habi-tation. God setteth the ... solitary in families: / he bringeth out those

which / are bound with chains: but the rebel-lious dwell in a dry … *land*. O God, when thou wentest forth / before thy people, when / thou didst march through the wilderness; Interlude:
The earth shook, the heavens also / dropped at the presence of / God: *even* Sinai itself / *was moved* at the presence … of God, the God of Israel. / Thou, O God, didst send a / plentiful rain, whereby thou didst / confirm thine inher'tance, … when it was weary. Thy congre-gation hath dwelt therein: / thou, O God, hast prepared of thy / goodness for the poor. The … Lord gave the word: great *was* the com-pany of those that pub-lished *it. The* Kings of armies did / flee apace: and she that … tarried at home divided the / spoil. Though ye have lien / among the pots, *yet shall ye be / as* the wings of a dove … covered with silver, and her fea-thers with yellow gold. When / the Almighty scattered kings in / it, it was *white* as snow … in Salmon. The hill of God *is / as* the hill of Bashan; / an high hill *as* the hill of Ba-shan. Why leap ye, ye high … why leap ye, ye high hills? *this is* / the hill *which* God desi-reth to dwell in; yea, the LORD will / dwell *in it* for ever. … The chariots of God *are* twen-ty thousand, *even* thou-sands of angels: the Lord *is* a-mong them, *as in* Sinai, … in the holy *place*. Thou hast as-cended on high, thou hast / led captivity captive: thou / hast received gifts for men; … yea, *for* the rebellious also, / that the LORD God might dwell / *among them.* Blessed *be* the Lord, / *who* daily loadeth us … *with benefits, even* the God / of our salvation. / Interlude.
He that is our God *is* the / God of salvation; and / unto GOD the Lord *belong* the / issues from death. But God … shall wound the head of his ene-mies, *and* the hairy scalp / of such an one as goeth on / still in his trespasses. … The Lord said, I will bring again / from Bashan, I will bring / *my people* again from the depths / of the sea: That thy foot … may be dipped in the blood of *thine* / enemies, *and* the tongue / of thy dogs in the same. They have / seen thy goings, O God; … *even* the goings of my God, / my King, in the sanct'ry. / The singers went before, *and* the / players on instruments … *followed* after; among *them were* / the damsels playing with / timbrels. Bless ye God in the con-gregations, *even* the … Lord,

from the fountain of Isra-el. There *is* little Ben-jamin *with* their ruler, the prin-ces of Judah *and* their ...council, the princes of Zebu-lun, *and* the princes of / Naphtali. Thy God hath comman-ded thy strength: strengthen, O ... God, that which thou hast wrought for us. / Because of thy temple / *there* at Jerusalem shall kings / bring presents unto thee. ... Rebuke the company of spear-men, *and* the multitude / of the bulls, with the calves of the / people, *till every one* ... submit himself with pieces of / silver: scatter thou the / people *that* delight in war. Prin-ces shall come from Egypt;... Ethiopia shall soon stretch out / her hands unto God. Sing / unto God, ye kingdoms of the / earth; O sing praises to ... the Lord; Interlude:
To him that rideth upon the / heavens of heavens, *which / were* of old; lo, he doth send out / his voice, a mighty voice. ... Ascribe ye strength unto God: his / excellency *is* ov'r / Israel, and his strength *is* in / the clouds. O God, *thou art* ... terrible out of thy holy / places: the God of Is-rael *is* he that giveth strength / and power unto *his* ... people. Blessed *be* God.

69   Psalm 69

To the chief Musician upon Shoshannim, *According to the Psalm* of David.

Save me, O God; for the waters / are come in unto *my* / soul. I sink in deep mire, where / *there is* no standing: I ... am come into deep waters, where / the floods overflow me. / I am weary of my crying: / my throat is dried: mine eyes ... fail while I wait for my God. They / that hate me without a / cause are more than the hairs of mine / head: they that would destroy ... me, *being* mine enemies wrong-fully, are mighty: then / I restored *that* which I took not / away. O God, thou know'st ... my foolishness; and my sins are / not hid from thee. Let not / them that wait on thee, O Lord GOD / of hosts, be ashamed for ... my sake: let not those that seek thee / be confounded for my / sake, O God of Israel. Be-cause for thy sake I have ... borne reproach; shame hath covered my / face. I am become a / stranger unto my brethren, and / an alien unto … my mother's children. For the zeal / of thine house hath eaten / me up; and the reproaches of / them that reproached thee are … fallen upon me. When I wept, / *and chastened* my soul with / fasting, that was to my reproach. / I made sackcloth also … my garment; and I became a / proverb to them. They that / sit in the gate speak against me; / and I *was* the song of … the drunkards. But as for me, my / prayer *is* unto thee, / O LORD, *in* an acceptable / time: O God, *and* in the … multitude of thy mercy hear / me, in the truth of thy / salvation. Deliver me out / of the mire, and let … me not sink: let me be deli-vered from them that hate me, / and out of the deep waters. *And* / let not the waterflood … overflow me, neither let the / deep swallow me up, and / let not the pit shut her mouth u-pon me. Hear me, O LORD; … for thy lovingkindness *is* good: / turn unto me accor-ding to the multitude of thy / tender mercies. And hide … not thy face from thy servant; for / I am in trouble: hear / me speedily. Draw nigh unto / my soul, *and* redeem it: … deliver me because of mine / enemies. Thou hast known / my reproach, and *hast known* my shame, / and my dishonour: mine … adversaries *are* all before / thee. Reproach hath broken / my heart; and I am full of hea-viness: and I looked *for* ... *some* to take pity, but *there was* / none; and for comforters, / but I found none. They gave me al-so gall for my meat; and … in my thirst they gave me vine-gar to drink. Let their ta-ble become a snare before them: / and *that which should have been* … for *their* welfare, *let it become* / a trap. Let their eyes be / darkened, that they see not; and make / their loins continually … to shake. Pour out thine indigna-tion upon them, and let / thy wrathful anger take hold of / them. Let their hab'tation … be desolate; *and* let none dwell / in their tents. For they per-secute *him* whom thou hast smitten; / and they talk to the grief … of those whom thou hast wounded. Add / iniquity unto / their iniquity: let them not / come to thy righteousness. … Let them be blotted out of the / book of the living, and / not be written with the righteous. / But I'*m* poor and sorr'wful: … let thy salvation, O God, set / me up on high. I will / praise the name of God with a song, / and will magnify him … with thanksgiving. *This* also shall / please the LORD better than / an ox *or* bullock that hath horns / and hoofs. The humble shall … see *this, and* be glad: and your heart / shall live that seek God. For / the LORD heareth the poor, and des-piseth not his pris'ners. … Let the heaven and earth praise him, / the seas, and every thing / that moveth therein. For God will / save Zion, and will build … the cities of Judah: that they / may dwell there, and have it / in possession. The seed also / of his servants *they* shall … inherit it: and they that love / his name shall dwell therein.

70   Psalm 70

To the chief Musician, *According to the Psalm* of David, to bring to remembrance.

Make haste, O God, to deliver / me; make haste to help me, / O LORD. Let them be ashamed and / confound'd that seek after … my soul: let them be turned backward, / and put to confusion, / that desire my hurt. *And* let / them be turned back for a … reward of their shame that say, A-ha, aha. Let all those / that seek thee rejoice and be glad / in thee: and let such as … love thy salvation say contin-u'lly, Let God be ma-gnified. But I *am* poor and nee-dy: make haste unto me, … O God: thou *art* my help and my / deliverer; O LORD, / make no tarrying.

71   Psalm 71

In thee, O LORD, do I put my / trust: let me never be / put to confusion. Deliver / me in thy righteousness, … and cause me to escape: incline / thine ear unto me, and / save me. Be thou my strong habi-tation, whereunto I … may continu'lly resort: thou / hast given commandment / to save me; for thou *art* my rock / and my fortress. Deliv'r … me, O my God, out of the hand / of the wicked, out of / the hand of the unrighteous and / cruel man. For thou *art* …

my hope, O Lord GOD: *thou art* my / trust from my youth. By thee / have I been holden up from the / womb: thou art he that took … me out of my mother's bow'ls: my / praise *shall be* continu'l-ly of thee. I am as a won-der unto many; but … thou *art* my strong refuge. Let my / mouth be filled *with* thy praise / *and with* thy honour all the day. / Cast me not off in the … time of old age; forsake me not / when my strength faileth. For / mine enemies speak against me; / and they that lay wait for … my soul take counsel together, / Saying, God hath forsa-ken him: persecute and take him; / for *there is* none to *help* … none to deliver *him.* O God, / be not far from me: O / my God, make haste for my help. Let / them be confounded *and* … consumed that are adversaries / to my soul; let them be / covered *with* reproach and disho-nour that seek my hurt. But … I will hope continu'lly, and / will yet praise thee more and / more. My mouth shall shew forth thy righ-teousness, thy salvation … all the day; for I know not the / numbers *thereof.* I will / go in the strength of the Lord GOD: / I will make mention of … thy righteousness, *even* of thine / only. O God, thou hast / taught me from my youth: and hither-to have I declared thy … wondrous works. Now also when I / am old and grayheaded, / O God, forsake me not; until / I have shewed thy strength to … *this* generation, *and* thy pow'r / to every one *that* is / to come. Thy righteousness also, / O God, *is* very high, … who hast done great things: O God, who / *is* like unto thee! *Thou,* / which hast shewed me great and sore trou-bles, shalt quicken me ' gain, … and shalt bring me up again from / the depths of the earth. Thou / shalt increase my greatness, and com-fort me on every side. … I will also praise thee with the / psalt'ry, *even* thy truth, / O my God: unto thee will I / sing with the harp, O thou … Holy One of Israel. My / lips shall greatly rejoice / when I sing unto thee; and my / soul, which thou hast redeemed. … My tongue also shall talk of thy / righteousness all the day / long: for they are confounded, for / they are brought unto shame, … that seek my hurt.

According to the Psalm for Solomon.

Give the king thy judgments, O God, / and thy righteousness un-to the king's son. He shall judge thy / people with righteousness, … and thy poor with judgment. The moun-tains shall bring peace to the / people, and the little hills, by / righteousness. He shall judge … the poor of the people, he shall / save the children of the / needy, and shall break in pieces / the oppressor. They shall … fear thee as long as the sun and / moon endure, throughout all / generations. He shall come down / like rain upon the mown … grass: as showers *that* water the / earth. In his days shall the / righteous flourish; and abundance / of peace so long as the … moon endureth. He shall have do-minion also from sea / to sea, and from the river unto / the ends of the earth. They … that dwell in the wilderness shall / bow before him; and his / enemies shall lick the dust. The / kings of Tarshish and of … the isles shall bring presents: the kings / of Sheba and Seba / shall offer gifts. Yea, all kings shall / fall down before him: all … nations shall serve him. For he shall / deliver the needy / when he cri'th; the poor also, and / *him* that hath no helper. … He shall spare the poor and needy, / and shall save the souls of / the needy. He shall redeem their / soul from deceit and *from* … violence: and precious shall their / blood be in his sight. And / he shall live, and to him shall be / given of the gold of … Sheba: pray'r also shall be made / for him continu'lly; / *and* daily shall he be praised. There / shall be an handful of … corn in the earth upon the top / of the mountains; the fruit / thereof shall shake like Lebanon: / and *they* of the city … shall flourish like grass of the earth. / His name shall endure for / ever: his name shall be contin-ued as long as the sun: … and *men* shall be blessed in him: all / nations shall call him bless'd. / Blessed *be* the LORD God, the God / of Israel, who doth … who only doeth wondrous things. / And blessed *be* his glo-rious name for ever: and let / the whole earth be filled *with* … his glory; Amen, and Amen.

The prayers of David the son of Jesse are ended.

73   Psalm 73

According to the Psalm of Asaph.

Truly God *is* good to Isr'el, / *even* to such as are / of a clean heart. But as for me, / my feet were almost gone; ... my steps had well nigh slipped. For I / was envious at the / foolish, *when* I saw the prospe-rity of the wicked. ... For *there are* no bands in their death: / but their strength *is* firm. They / *are* not in trouble *as other* / men; neither are they plagued ... like *other* men. Therefore pride com-passeth them about as / a chain; violence covereth / them *as* a garment. Their ... eyes stand out with fatness: they have / more than heart could wish. They / are corrupt, and speak wickedly / *concerning* oppression: ...they speak loftily. They set their / mouth against the heavens, / and their tongue walketh through the earth. / Therefore his people turn ... hither: and waters of a full / *cup* are wrung out to them. / And they say, How doth God know? and / is there knowledge in the ... most High? Behold, these *are* the un-godly, who prosper in / the world; they increase *in* riches. / Verily I have cleansed ... my heart *in* vain, and washed my hands / in innocency. For / all the day long have I been plagued, / chastened every morning. ... If I say, I will speak thus; be-hold, I should offend *a-gainst* the generation of thy / children. When I thought to ... know this, *then* it *was* too painful / for me; Until I went / into the sanct'ry of God; *and* / *then* understood I their ... end. Surely thou didst set them in / slipp'ry places: thou cas-tedst them down into destruction. / How are they *brought* into ... desolation, as in a mo-ment! they are utterly / consumed with terrors. As a dream / when *one* awaketh; *so*, ... O Lord, when thou awakest, thou / shalt despise their image. / Thus my heart was grieved, and I was / pricked in my reins. Foolish, ... so foolish *was* I, and igno-rant: I was *as* a beast / before thee. Nevertheless I / *am* continu'lly with ... thee: thou hast holden *me* by my / right hand. Thou shalt guide me / with thy counsel, and afterward / receive me *to* glory. ... Whom have I in heaven *but thee*? / and *there is* none upon / earth *that* I desire beside / thee. My flesh and my heart ... faileth: *but* God *is* the strength of / my heart, and my portion / for ever. For, lo, they that are / far from thee shall perish: ... thou hast destroyed all them that go / a whoring from thee. But / *it is* good for me to draw near / to God: I have put my ... trust in the Lord GOD, that I may / declare all thy works.

74   Psalm 74

According to the Maschil of Asaph.

O God, why hast thou cast *us* off / for ever? *why* doth thine / anger smoke against the sheep of / thy pasture? Remember ... thy congregation, *which* thou hast / purchased of old; the rod / of thine 'heritance, *which* thou hast / redeemed; this mount Zion, ... wherein thou hast dwelt. Lift up thy / feet unto the perpe-tual desolations; *even* / all *that* the enemy ... hath done wickedly in the sanc-tuary. Thine ene-mies roar in the midst of thy con-gregations; they set up ... their ensigns *for* signs. *A man* was / famous according as / he had lifted up axes u-pon the thick trees. But now ... they break down the carved work thereof / at once with axes and / hammers. They have cast fire in-to thy sanctuary, ... they have defiled *by casting down* / the dwelling place of thy / name to the ground. They said in their / hearts, Let us destroy them ... together: they have burned up all / the synagogues of God / in the land. *And* we see not o-ur signs: *there is* no more ... any prophet: neither *is there* / among us any that / knoweth how long. O God, how long / shall the adversary ... reproach? shall the enemy blas-pheme thy name for ever? / Why withdrawest thou thy hand, e-ven thy right hand? pluck *it* ... out of thy bosom. For God *is* / my King of old, working / salvation in the midst of the / earth. Thou didst divide the ... sea by thy strength: thou brakest the / heads of the dragons in / the waters. Thou brakest the heads / of leviathan in ... pieces, *and* gavest him *to be* / meat to the people in-habiting the wilderness. Thou / didst cleave the fountain and ... the flood: thou driedst up mighty / rivers. The day *is* thine, / the night also *is* thine: thou hast / prepared the light and the ... sun. Thou hast set all the borders / of the earth: thou hast made / summer and winter. Remember / this, *that* the enemy ... hath reproached, O LORD, and *that* the / foolish people have blasphemed thy name. O deliver not / the soul of thy turtle-dove unto the multitude *of / the wicked*: forget not / the congregation of thy poor / for ever. Have respect ... unto the covenant: for the / dark places of the earth / are full of the habitations / of cruelty. O let ... not the oppressed return ashamed: / let the poor and needy / praise thy name. Arise, O God, plead / thine own cause: remember ... how the foolish man reproacheth / thee daily. Forget not / the voice of thine enemies: the / tumult of those that rise ... up against thee increaseth con-tinually.

75   **Psalm 75**

To the chief Musician, Al-taschith, *According to the* Psalm *or* Song of Asaph.

Unto thee, O God, do we give / thanks, *unto thee* do we / give thanks: for *that* thy name is near / thy wondrous works declare. ... When I shall receive the congre-gation I will judge up-rightly. The earth and all the in-habitants thereof are ... dissolved: I bear up the pillars / of it. Interlude.
I said unto the fools, Deal not / foolishly: and to the / wicked, Lift not up the horn: Lift / not up your horn on high: ... speak *not with* a stiff neck. For pro-motion *cometh* neither / from the east, nor from the west, nor / from the south. But God *is* ... the judge: he putteth down one, and / setteth up another. / For in the hand of the LORD *there / is* a cup, and the wine ... is red; it is full of mixture; / and he poureth out of / the same: but the dregs thereof, all / the wicked of the earth ... shall wring *them* out, *and* drink *them*. But / I will declare for ev'r; / I will sing praises to the God / of Jacob. All the

horns … of the wicked also will I / cut off; *but* the horns of / the righteous shall be exalted.

76   **Psalm 76**

To the chief Musician on Neginoth, *According to the* Psalm *or* Song of Asaph.

In Judah *is* God known: his name / *is* great in Israel. / In Salem also is his ta-bernacle, his dwelling … place in Zion. There brake he the / arrows of the bow, the / shield, and the sword, and the battle. Interlude.
Thou *art* more glorious *and* ex-cellent than the mountains / of prey. The stouthearted are spoiled, / they have slept their sleep: and … none of the men of might have found / their hands. At thy rebuke, / O God of Jacob, both the cha-riot and horse are cast … into a dead sleep. Thou, *even* / thou, *art* to be feared: and / who may stand in thy sight when once / thou art angry? Thou didst … cause judgment to be heard from hea-ven; the earth feared, and was / still, When God arose to judgment, / to save all the meek of … the earth. Interlude.
Surely the wrath of man shall praise / thee: the remainder of / wrath shalt thou restrain. Vow, and pay / unto the LORD your God: … let all that be round about him / bring presents unto him / that ought to be feared. He shall cut / off the spirit of princ's: … *he is* terrible to the kings / of the earth.

77   **Psalm 77**

To the chief Musician, to Jeduthun, *According to the* Psalm of Asaph.

I cried unto God with my voice, / *even* unto God with / my voice; and he gave ear unto / me. In the day of my … trouble I sought the

Lord: my sore / ran in the night, and ceased / not: my soul refused to be com-forted. I remembered ... God, and was troubled: I complained, / and my spirit was o-verwhelmed. Interlude.

Thou holdest mine eyes waking: I / am so troubled that I / cannot speak. I have considered / the days of old, the years ... of ancient times. I call to re-membrance my song in the / night: I commune with mine own heart: / my spirit made dil'gent ... search. Will the Lord cast off for e-ver? and will he be fa-v'rable no more? Is his mercy / clean gone for ever? doth ... *his* promise fail for evermore? / Hath God forgotten to / be gracious? hath he in anger / shut up his tend'r mercies? Interlude.

And I said, This *is* my infir-mity: *but I will re-member* the years of the right hand / of the most High. I will ... remember the works of the LORD: / surely I will remem-ber thy wonders of old. I will / meditate also of ... all thy work, and talk of thy do-ings. Thy way, O God, *is* / in the sanctuary: who *is* / *so* great a God as *our* ... God? Thou *art* the God that doest / wonders: thou hast declared / thy strength among the people. Thou / hast with *thine* arm redeemed ... thy people, the sons of Jacob / and Joseph. Interlude.

The waters saw thee, O God, the / waters saw thee; they were / afraid: *and* the depths also were / troubled. The clouds poured out ... water: the skies sent out a sound: / thine arrows also went / abroad. The voice of thy thunder / *was* in the heaven: the ... lightnings lightened the world: the earth / trembled and shook. Thy way / *is* in the sea, and thy path in / the great waters, and thy ... footsteps are not known. Thou leddest / thy people like a flock / by the hand of Moses and Aa-ron.

78 (1)   **Psalm 78**

According to the Maschil of Asaph.

Give ear, O my people, *to* my / law: incline your ears to / the words of my mouth. I'll open / my mouth in a par'ble: ... I will utter dark sayings of / old: Which we have heard and / known, and o'r fathers have told us. / We will not hide *them* from … their children, shewing to the ge-neration to come the / praises of the LORD, and his strength, / and his wonderful works … that he hath done. For he esta-blished a testimony / in Jacob, and appointed a / law in Israel, which … he commanded our fathers, that / they should make them known to / their children: That the genera-tion to come might know *them, … even* the children *which* should be / born; *who* should arise and / declare *them* to their children: That / they might set their hope in … God, and not forget the works of / God, but keep his command-ments: And might not be as their fa-thers, a stubborn and *a* … rebellious generation; a / generation *that* set / not their heart aright, and whose spi-rit was not stedfast with … God. The children of Ephraim, / *being* armed, carry'ng bows, / turned back in the day of battle. / They kept not the cov'nant … of God, and refused to walk in / his law; And forgat his / works, and his wonders that he had / shewed them. Marvellous things … did he in the sight of their fa-thers, in the land of E-gypt, *in* the field of Zoan. He / divided the sea, and … caused them to pass through; and he made / the waters to stand as / an heap. In the daytime also / he led them with a cloud, … and all the night with a light of / fire. He clave the rocks / in the wilderness, and gave *them* / drink as *out of* the great … depths. He brought streams also out of / the rock, and caused waters / to run down like rivers. And they / sinned yet more against him … by provoking the most High in / the wilderness. And they / tempted God in their heart by as-king meat for their lust. Yea, … they spake against God; they said, Can / God furnish a table / in the wilderness? Behold, he / smote the rock, *so* that the … waters gushed out, and the streams o-verflowed; can he give bread / also? can he provide flesh for / his people? Therefore the … LORD heard *this*, and was wroth: so a / fire was kindled a-gainst Jacob, and anger also / came up against Isr'el; … Because they believed not in God, / and trusted not in his / salvation: Though he had comman-ded the clouds from above, … and opened the doors of heaven, / And had rained down manna / upon them to eat, and had gi-ven them of the corn of … heaven. Man did eat angels' food: / he sent them meat to the / full. He caused an east wind to blow / in the heaven: and by … his power he brought in the south / wind. He rained flesh also / upon them as dust, and feathered / fowls like as the sand of … the sea: And he let *it* fall in / the midst of their camp, round / about their habitations. So / they did eat, and were well … filled: for he gave them their own de-sire; They were not e-stranged from their lust. But while their meat / *was* yet in their mouths, The … wrath of God came upon them, and / slew the fattest of them, / and smote down the chosen *men* of / Israel. For all this … they sinned still, and believed not for / his wondrous works. Therefore / their days did he consume in va-nity, and their years in … trouble. When he slew them, then they / sought him: and they returned / and inquired early after / God. And they remembered … that God *was* their rock, and the high / God their redeemer. Ne-vertheless they did flatter him / with their mouth, and they lied … unto him with their tongues. For their / heart was not right with him, / neither were they stedfast in his / cov'nant. But he, *being* … full of compassion, forgave *their* / iniquity, and de-stroyed *them* not: yea, many a time / turned he his anger 'way, … and did not stir up all his wrath. / For he remembered that / they *were but* flesh; a wind that pas-seth away, and cometh … not again. How oft did they pro-voke him in the wilder-ness, *and* grieve him in the desert! / Yea, they turned back and tempt'd … God, and limited the Holy / One of Israel. They / remembered not his hand, *nor* the / day when he delivered … them from the enemy.

78 (2) **Psalm 78**

Israel remembered not how / he had wrought his signs in / Egypt, and his wonders in the / field of Zoan: And had … turned their rivers into blood; and / their floods, that they could not / drink. He sent divers sorts of flies / among them, which devour'd … them; and frogs, which destroyed them. He / gave also their increase / unto the caterpiller, and / their labour unto the … locust. He destroyed their vines with / hail, and their sycomore / trees with frost. He gave up their cat-tle also to the hail, ... and their flocks to hot thunderbolts. / He cast upon them the / fierceness of his anger, wrath, and / indignation, trouble, ... by sending evil angels *a-mong them*. He made a way / to his anger; he spared not their / soul from death, but gave their ... life over to the pestilence; / And smote all the firstborn / in Egypt; the chief of *their* strength / in the tabernacles ... of Ham: But made his own people / to go forth like sheep, and / guided them in the wilderness / like a flock. And he led ... them on safely, so that they feared / not: but the sea over-whelmed their enemies. And he brought / them to the border of ... his sanctuary, *even to* / this mountain, *which* his right / hand had purchased. He cast out the / heathen also before ... them, and divided them an in-heritance by line, and / made the tribes of Israel to / dwell in their tents. Yet they ...tempted and provoked the most high / God, and kept not his tes-timonies: But turned back, and dealt / unfaithfully like their ... fathers: they were turned aside like / a deceitful bow. For / they provoked him to anger with / their high places, and moved ... him to jealousy with their gra-ven images. When God / heard *this*, he was wroth, and greatly / abhorred Israel: So ... that he forsook the taberna-cle of Shiloh, the tent / *which* he placed among men; And de-livered his strength into ... captivity, and his glory / into the enemy's / hand. He gave his people over / also unto the sword; ... and was wroth with his inheri-tance. The fire consumed / their young men; and their maidens were / not given to marriage. ... Their priests fell by the sword; and their / widows made no lamen-tation. Then the Lord awaked as / one out of sleep, *and* like ... a mighty man that shouteth by / reason of wine. And he / smote his enemies in the hin-der parts: he put them to ... a perpetual reproach. More-over he refused the / tabernacle of Joseph, and / *he* chose not the tribe of ... Ephraim: But chose the tribe of / Judah, the mount Zion / which he loved. And he built his sanc-tu'ry like high *palac's*, ... like the earth which he hath esta-blished for ever. He chose / David also his servant, and / took him from the sheepfolds: ... From following the ewes great with / young he brought him to feed / Jacob his people, and Isra-el his inheritance. ... So he fed

them according to / the integrity of / his heart; and guided them by
the / skilfulness of his hands.

79   **Psalm 79**

According to the Psalm of Asaph.

O God, the heathen are come to / thine inheritance; thy / holy
temple have they defiled; / they have laid J'rusalem … on heaps.
The dead bodies of thy / servants have they given / *to be* meat unto
the fowls of / the heaven, the flesh of … thy saints unto the beasts of
the / earth. Their blood have they shed / like water round about Jerusalem; and *there was* none … to bury *them*. We are become / a
reproach to our neigh-bours, a scorn and derision to / them that are
round about … us. How long, LORD? wilt thou be an-gry for ever?
shall thy / jealousy burn like fire? Pour / out thy wrath upon the …
heathen that have not known thee, and / upon the kingdoms that /
have not called upon thy name. For / they have devour'd Jacob, …
and laid waste his dwelling place. O / remember not against / us
former iniquities: *and* / let thy tender mercies … speedily prevent
us: for we / are brought very low. Help / us, O God of our salvation, for the glory of … thy name: and deliver us, and / purge away
our sins, / for thy name's sake. Wherefore should the / heathen say,
Where *is* their … God? let him be known among the / heathen in
our sight / *by* the revenging of the blood / of thy servants *which is*
… shed. Let the sighing of the pri-soner come before thee; /
according to the greatness of / thy power preserve thou … those that
are appointed to die; / And render unto our / neighbours sevenfold
into their / bosom their reproach, where-with they have reproached
thee, O Lord. / So we thy people and / sheep of thy pasture will give
thee / thanks for ever: we will … shew forth thy praise to all generations.

To the chief Musician upon Shoshannim-Eduth, *According to the* Psalm of Asaph.

Give ear, O Shepherd of Isra-el, thou that leadest Jo-seph like a flock; thou that dwellest / *between* the cherubims, ... shine forth. Before Ephraim and / Benjamin and Manas-seh stir up thy strength, and come *and* / save us. Turn us again, ... O God, and cause thy face to shine; / and we shall be saved. O / LORD God of hosts, how long wilt thou / be angry against the ... prayer of thy people? Thou fee-dest them with the bread of / tears; and givest them tears to drink / in great measure. Thou mak'st ... us a strife to our neighbours: and / our enemies laugh / among themselves. Turn us again, / O God of hosts, and cause ... thy face to shine; and we shall be / saved. Thou hast brought a vine / out of Egypt: thou hast cast out / the heathen, and planted ... it. Thou preparedst *room* before / it, and didst cause it to / take deep root, and it filled the land. / The hills were covered with ... the shadow of it, and the boughs / thereof *were like* the goo-dly cedars. She sent out her boughs / unto the sea, and her ... branches unto the river. Why / hast thou *then* broken down / her hedges, so that all they which / pass by the way do pluck ... her? The boar out of the wood doth / waste it, and the wild beast / of the field doth devour it. / Return, we beseech thee, ... O God of hosts: look down from hea-ven, and behold, and vi-sit this vine; And the vineyard which / thy right hand hath planted, ... and the branch *that* thou madest strong / for thyself. *It is* burned / with fire, *it is* cut down: they / perish at the rebuke ... of thy countenance. Let thy hand / be upon the man of / thy right hand, upon the son of / man *whom* thou madest strong ... for thyself. So will not we go / back from thee: quicken us, / and we will call upon thy name. / Turn us again, O LORD ... God of hosts, cause thy face to shine; / and we shall be saved.

To the chief Musician upon Gittith, *According to the Psalm* of Asaph.

Sing aloud unto God our strength: / make a joyful noise un-to the God of Jacob. Take a / psalm, and bring hither the … timbrel, the pleasant harp with the / psalt'ry. Blow up the trum-pet in the new moon, in the time / appointed, on our sol'mn … feast day. For this *was* a statute / for Israel, *and* a / law of the God of Jacob. This / he ordained in Joseph … *for* a testimony, when he / went out through the land of / Egypt: *where* I heard a language / *that* I understood not. … I removed his shoulder from the / burden: his hands were de-livered from the pots. Thou call'dst in / trouble, I deliver'd … I delivered thee; I answered / thee in the secret place / of thunder: I proved thee at the / waters of Meribah. Interlude.
Hear, O my people, and I will / testify unto thee: / O Israel, if thou wilt hear-ken unto me; There shall … no strange god be in thee; neither / shalt thou worship any / strange god. I *am* the LORD thy God, / which brought thee out of the … land of Egypt: open thy mouth / wide, and I will fill it. / But my people would not hearken / to my voice; and Isr'el … would none of me. So I gave them / up unto their own hearts' / lust: *and* they walked in their own coun-sels. Oh that my people … had hearkened unto me, *and* Is-rael had walked in my / ways! I should soon have subdued their / enemies, and turned my … hand against their adversaries. / The haters of the LORD / should have submitted themselves un-to him: but their time should …have endured for ever. He should / have fed them also with / the finest of the wheat: and with / honey out of the rock … should I have satisfied thee.

82   Psalm 82

According to the Psalm of Asaph.

God standeth in the congrega-tion of the mighty; he / judgeth among the gods. How long / will ye judge unjustly, ... and accept the persons of the / wicked? Interlude.
Defend the poor and fatherless: / do justice to the af-flicted and needy. Deliver / the poor and needy: rid ... *them* out of the hand of the wi-cked. They know not, neither / will they understand; they walk on / in darkness: *and* all the ... foundations of the earth are out / of course. I have said, Ye / *are* gods; and all of you *are* chil-dren of the most High. But ... ye shall die like men, fall like one / of the princes. Arise, / O God, judge the earth: for thou shalt / inherit all nations.

83   Psalm 83

According to the Song *or* Psalm of Asaph.

Keep not thou silence, O God: hold / not thy peace, and be not / still, O God. For, lo, thine ene-mies make a tumult: and ... they that hate thee have lifted up / the head. They have taken / crafty counsel against thy peo-ple, and *have* consulted ... against thy hidden ones. They have / said, Come, and let us cut / them off from *being* a nation; / that the name of Isr'el ... may be no more in remembrance. / For they have consulted / together with one consent: *and* / they are confederate ... against thee: The tabernacles / of Edom, and the Ish-maelites; of Moab, and the / Hagaren's; Gebal, and ... Ammon, and Amalek; the Phi-listines with the inha-bitants of Tyre; Assur al-so is joined with them: they ... have holpen the children of Lot. Interlude.
Do unto them as *unto* the / Midianites; as *to* / Sisera, as *to* Jabin, at / the brook of Kison: *Which* ... perished at En-dor: they became / *as* dung for the earth. Make / their nobles like Oreb, and like / Zeeb: yea, all their princ's ... as Zebah, and as Zalmunna: / Who said, Let

us take to / ourselves the houses of God in / possession. O my God, …make them like a wheel; as the stub-ble before the wind. As / the fire burneth a wood, and / as the flame setteth the … mountains on fire; So perse-cute them with thy tempest, / and make them afraid with thy storm. / Fill their faces with shame; … that they may seek thy name, O LORD. / Let them be confounded / and troubled for ever; yea, let / them be put to shame, and … perish: That *men* may know that thou, / whose name alone *is* JE-HOVAH, *art* the most high over / all the earth.

84   Psalm 84

To the chief Musician upon Gittith, *According to the* Psalm for the sons of Korah.

How amiable *are* thy taber-nacles, O LORD of hosts! / My soul longeth, yea, even fain-teth for the courts of the … LORD: my heart and my flesh crieth / out for the living God. / Yea, the sparrow hath found an house, / and the swallow a nest … for herself, where she may lay her / young, *even* thine altars, / O LORD of hosts, my King, and my / God. Blessed *are* they that … dwell in thy house: they will be still / praising thee. Interlude.
Blessed *is* the man whose strength *is* / in thee; in whose heart *are* / the ways *of them. Who* passing through / the valley of Baca … make it a well; the rain also / filleth the pools. They go / from strength to strength, *every one of* / *them* in Zion appear'th … before God. O LORD God of hosts, / hear my prayer: give ear, / O God of Jacob. Interlude.
Behold, O God our shield, and / look upon the face of / thine anointed. For a day in / thy courts *is* better than … a thousand. I had rather be / a doorkeeper in the / house of my God, than to dwell in / the tents of wickedness. … For the LORD God *is* a sun and / shield: the LORD will give grace / and glory: no good *thing* will he / withhold from them that walk … uprightly. O LORD of hosts, bles-sed *is* the man that trus-teth in thee.

85   Psalm 85

To the chief Musician, *According to the* Psalm for the sons of Korah.

LORD, thou hast been favourable / unto thy land: thou hast / brought back the captivity of / Jacob. Thou hast forgiv'n … the iniquity of thy peo-ple, thou hast covered all / their sin. Interlude. Thou hast taken away all thy / wrath: thou hast turned *thyself* / from the fierceness of thine anger. / Turn us, O God of our … salvation, and cause thine anger / toward us to cease. Wilt / thou be angry with us for e-ver? wilt thou draw out thine … anger to all generations? / Wilt thou not revive us / again: that thy people may re-joice in thee? Shew us thy … mercy, O LORD, and grant us thy / salvation. I will hear / what God the LORD will speak: for he / will speak peace unto his … people, and to his saints: but let / them not turn again to / folly. Surely his salvation / *is* nigh them that fear him; … that glory may dwell in our land. / Mercy and truth are met / together; righteousness and peace / have kissed *each other*. Truth … shall spring out of the earth; and righ-teousness shall look down from / heaven. Yea, the LORD shall give *that / which is* good; and our land … shall yield her increase. Righteousness / shall go before him; and / shall set *us* in the way of his / steps.

86   Psalm 86

According to the Prayer of David.

Bow down thine ear, O LORD, hear me: / for I *am* poor and nee-dy. Preserve my soul; for I *am* / holy: O thou my God, … save thy servant that trusteth in / thee. Be merciful un-to me, O Lord: for I cry un-to thee daily. Rejoice … the soul of thy servant: for un-to thee, O Lord, do I / lift up my soul. For thou, Lord, *art* / good, and *art* ready to … forgive; and plenteous in mercy / unto all them that call / upon thee. Give ear, O LORD, to / my prayer; and attend … to the voice of my supplica-tions. In the day of my / trouble I will call upon thee: / for thou wilt answer me. … Among the gods *there is* none like / unto thee, O Lord; nei-ther *are there any works* like un-to thy works. All nations … whom thou hast made shall come and wor-ship before thee, O Lord; / and shall glorify thy name. For / thou *art* great, and doest … wondrous things: thou *art* God alone. / Teach me thy way, O LORD; / I will walk in thy truth: unite / my heart to fear thy name. … I will praise thee, O Lord my God, / with all my heart: and I / will glorify thy name for e-vermore. For great *is* thy … mercy toward me: and thou hast / delivered my soul from / the lowest hell. O God, the proud / are risen against me, … and the assemblies of vi'lent / *men* have sought after my / soul; and have not set thee before / them. But thou, O Lord, *art* … a God full of compassion, and / gracious, longsuffering, / and plenteous in mercy and truth. / O turn unto me, and … have mercy upon me; give thy / strength unto thy servant, / and save the son of thine handmaid. / Shew me a token for … good; that they which hate me may see / *it,* and be ashamed: be-cause thou, LORD, hast holpen me, and / comforted me.

87   Psalm 87

According to the Psalm *or* Song for the sons of Korah.

His foundation *is* in the ho-ly mountains. The LORD lo-veth the gates of Zion more than / all the dwellings Jacob's. … Glorious things are spoken of / thee, O city of God. Interlude.
I will make mention of Rahab / and Babylon to them / that know me: behold Philisti-a, and Tyre, *and* with … Ethiopia; this *man* was born / there. And of Zion it / shall be said, This and that man was / born in her: and the high'st … the highest himself shall esta-blish her. The LORD shall count, / when he writeth up the people, / *that* this *man* was born there. Interlude.
As well the singers as the play-ers on instruments *shall / be there*: all my springs *are* in thee.

According to the Song *or* Psalm for the sons of Korah, to the chief Musician upon Mahalath Leannoth, Maschil of Heman the Ezrahite.

O LORD God of my salvation, / I have cried day *and* night / before thee: Let my prayer come / before thee: incline thine … ear unto my cry; For my soul / is full of troubles: and / my life draweth nigh unto the / grave. I am counted with … them that go down into the pit: / I am as a man *that / hath* no strength: Free among the dead, / like the slain that lie in … the grave, whom thou rememb'rest no / more: and they are cut off / from thy hand. Thou hast laid me in / the lowest pit, in dark … Thou hast laid me in darkness, in / the deeps. Thy wrath lieth / hard on me, and thou hast afflic-ted *me* with all thy waves. …Interlude.

Thou hast put away mine acquain-tance far from me; thou hast / made me an abomination / unto them: *I am* shut … up, and I cannot come forth. Mine / eye mourneth by reason / of affliction: LORD, I have called / daily upon thee, I … have stretched out my hands unto thee. / Wilt thou shew wonders to / the dead? shall the dead arise *and* / praise thee? Interlude.

Shall thy lovingkindness be de-clared in the grave? *or* thy / faithfulness in destruction? Shall / thy wonders be known in … the dark? and thy righteousness in / the land of forgetful-ness? But unto thee have I cried, / O LORD; in the morning … shall my prayer prevent thee. LORD, / why castest thou off my / soul? *why* hidest thou thy face from / me? I *am* afflicted … and ready to die from *my* youth / up: *while* I suffer thy / terrors I am distracted. Thy / fierce wrath goeth over … me; thy terrors have cut me off. / They came round about me / daily like water; they compassed / me about together. … Lover and friend hast thou put far / from me, *and* mine acquain-tance into darkness.

According to the Maschil of Ethan the Ezrahite.

I will sing of the mercies of / the LORD for ever: *and* / with my mouth will I make known thy / faithfulness to all *the* … generations. For I have said, / Mercy shall be built up / for ever: thy faithfulness shalt / thou establish in the … very heavens. I have made a / covenant with my cho-sen, I have sworn unto David / my servant, Thy seed will … I establish for ever, and / build up thy throne to all / generations. Interlude.
And the heavens shall praise thy won-ders, O LORD: thy faithful-ness also in the congrega-tion of the saints. For who … in the heaven can be compared / unto the LORD? *who* a-mong the sons of the mighty can / be likened unto the … LORD? God is greatly to be feared / in the assembly of / the saints, and to be had in re-verence of all *them that* … *are* about him. O LORD God of / hosts, who *is* a strong LORD / like unto thee? or to thy faith-fulness round about thee? … Thou rulest the raging of the / sea: when the waves thereof / arise, thou stillest them. Thou hast / broken Rahab in piec's, … as one that is slain; thou hast scat-tered thine enemies with / thy strong arm. The heavens *are* thine, / the earth also *is* thine: … *as for* the world and the fulness / thereof, thou hast founded / them. The north and the south thou hast / created them: Tabor … and Hermon shall rejoice in thy / name. Thou hast a mighty / arm: strong is thy hand, *and* high is / thy right hand. Justice and … judgment *are* the habitation / of thy throne: mercy and / truth shall go before thy face. Bles-sed *is* the people that … know the joyful sound: they shall walk, / O LORD, in the light of / thy countenance. In thy name shall / they rejoice all the day: … and in thy righteousness shall they / be exalted. For thou / *art* the glory of their strength: and / in thy favour our horn … shall be exalted. For the LORD / *is* our defence; and / the Holy One of Israel / *is* our king. Then thou … spakest in vision to thy ho-ly one, and saidst, I have / laid help upon *one that is* migh-ty; I have exalted … *one*

chosen out of the people. / I have found David my / servant; with my holy oil have / I anointed him: With … whom my hand shall be established: / mine arm also shall streng-then him. The enemy shall not / exact upon him; nor … the son of wickedness afflict / him. And I will beat down / his foes before his face, and plague / them that hate him. But my … faithfulness and my mercy *shall / be* with him: and in my / name shall his horn be exalted. / I'll set his hand also … in the sea, and his right hand in / the rivers. He shall cry / unto me, Thou *art* my father, / my God, and the rock of … my salvation. Also I will / make him *my* firstborn, high-er than the kings of the earth. My / mercy will I keep for … him for evermore, and my co-venant shall stand fast with / him. His seed also will I make / *to endure* for ever, …and his throne as the days of hea-ven. If his children for-sake my law, and walk not in my / judgments; If they break my … statutes, and keep not my command-ments; Then will I visit / their transgression with the rod, and / their iniquity with … stripes. Nevertheless my loving-kindness will I not ut-terly take from him, nor suffer / my faithfulness to fail. … My covenant will I not break, / nor alter the thing that / is gone out of my lips. Once have / I sworn by my holy … by my holiness that I will / not lie unto David. / His seed shall endure for ever, / and his throne as the sun … as the sun before me. It shall / be established for e-ver as the moon, and *as* a faith-ful witness in heaven. Interlude.

But thou hast cast off and abhorred, / thou hast been wroth with thine / anointed. *And* thou hast made void / the covenant of thy … servant: thou hast profaned his crown / *by casting it* to the / ground. Thou hast broken down all his / hedges; thou hast brought his / strong holds to ruin. All that pass / by the way spoil him: he / is a reproach to his neighbours. / Thou hast set up the right … hand of his adversaries; thou / hast made all his en'mies / to rejoice. Thou hast also turned / the edge of his sword, and … hast not made him to stand in the / battle. Thou hast made his / glory to cease, and cast his throne / down to the ground. The days … of his youth hast thou shortened: thou / hast covered him with shame. Interlude.

How long, LORD? wilt thou hide thyself / for ever? shall thy wrath / burn like fire? Remember how / short my time is: wherefore … hast thou made all men in vain? What / man *is he that* liveth, / and shall not see death? shall he de-liver his soul from the … hand of the grave? Interlude.

Lord, where *are* thy former loving-kindnesses, *which* thou swa-rest unto David in thy truth? / *And* remember, Lord, the … reproach of thy servants; *how* I / do bear in my bosom / *the reproach of* all the mighty / people; Wherewith *they,* thine … enemies have reproached, O LORD; / wherewith they have reproached / the footsteps of thine anointed. / Blessed *be* the LORD for … evermore. Amen, and Amen.

90   Psalm 90

According to the Prayer of Moses the man of God.

Lord, thou hast been our dwelling place / in all generations. / Before the mountains were brought forth, / or ever thou hadst formed … the earth and the world, even from / everlasting to e-verlasting, thou *art* God. Thou tur-nest man to destruction; … and sayest, Return, ye children / of men. For a thousand / years in thy sight *are but* as yes-terday when it is past, … and *as* a watch in the night. Thou / carriest them away / as with a flood; they are *as* a / sleep: in the morning *they* … *are* like grass *which* groweth up. In / the morning it flouri-sheth, and groweth up; in the e-vening it is cut down, … and wither'th. For we are consumed / by thine anger, and by / thy wrath are we troubled. Thou hast / set o'r iniquities … before thee, our secret *sins* / in the light of thy coun-tenance. For all o'r days are passed / away in thy wrath: we … spend our years as a tale *that / is told.* The days of our / years *are* threescore years and ten; and / if by reason of strength / *they be* fourscore years, yet *is* their / strength labour and sorrow; / for it is soon cut off, and we / fly away. Who knoweth … the power of thine anger? e-ven according to thy / fear, *so is* thy wrath. So teach *us* / to number our days, … that we may apply *our* hearts / unto wisdom. Return, / O LORD, how long? and let it re-pent thee concerning thy … servants. O satisfy us ear-ly with thy mercy; that / we may rejoice and be glad all / our days. Make us glad … according to the days *wherein* / thou hast afflicted us, / *and* the years *wherein* we have seen / evil. Let thy work 'pear … unto thy servants, and thy glo-ry unto their children. / And let the beauty of the LORD / our God be upon us: … and establish thou the work of / our hands upon us; yea, / the work of our hands esta-blish thou it.

91   **Psalm 91**

He that dwelleth in the secret / place of the most High shall / abide under the shadow of / the Almighty. I will … say of the LORD, *He is* my re-fuge and my fortress: my / God; in him will I trust. Surely / he shall deliver thee … from the snare of the fowler, *and* / from the noisome pesti-lence. He shall cover thee with his / feathers, and under his … wings shalt thou trust: his truth *shall be / thy* shield and buckler. Thou / shalt not be afraid for the ter-ror by night; *nor* for the … arrow *that* flieth by day; *Nor* / for the pestilence *that* / walketh in darkness; *nor* for the / destruction *that* wasteth … at noonday. A thousand shall fall / at thy side, and ten thou-sand at thy right hand; *but* it shall / not come nigh thee. Only … with thine eyes shalt thou behold and / see the reward of the / wicked. Because thou hast made the / LORD, *which is* my refuge, … *even* the most High, thy habi-tation; There shall no e-vil b'fall thee, neither shall any / plague come nigh thy dwelling. … For he shall give his angels charge / over thee, to keep thee / in all thy ways. They shall bear thee / up in *their* hands, lest thou … dash thy foot against a stone. *And* / thou shalt tread upon the / lion and adder: the young li-on and the dragon shalt … thou trample under feet. Because / he hath set his love u-pon me, therefore will I deli-ver him: I will set him … on high, because he hath known my / name. He shall call upon / me, and I will answer him: I / *will be* with him *there* in … trouble; I will deliver him, / and honour him. With long / life will I satisfy him, and / shew him my salvation.

92   **Psalm 92**

According to a Psalm *or* Song for the sabbath day.

It is a good *thing* to give thanks / unto the LORD, and to / sing praises unto thy name, O / most High: To shew forth thy … lovingkindness in the morning, / and thy faithfulness e-very night, Upon an instrument / of ten strings, and upon … the psalt'ry; upon the harp with / a solemn sound. For thou, / LORD, hast made me glad through thy work: / I will triumph in the … works of thy hands. O LORD, how great / are thy works! *and* thy thoughts / are very deep. A brutish man / knoweth not; neither doth … a fool understand this. When the / wicked spring as the grass, / and when all the workers of in-iquity do flourish; … *it is* that they shall be destroyed / for ever: But thou, LORD, / *art most* high for evermore. For, / lo, thine enemies, O … LORD, for, lo, thine enemies shall / perish; all the workers / of iniquity shall be scat-tered. But my horn shalt thou … exalt like *the horn of* an u-nicorn: I shall be a-nointed with fresh oil. Mine eye al-so shall see *my desire* … on mine enemies, *and* mine ears / shall hear *my desire* / of the wicked that rise up a-gainst me. The righteous shall … flourish like the palm tree: he shall / grow like a cedar in / Lebanon. Those that be planted / in the house of the LORD … shall flourish in the courts of our / God. They shall still bring forth / fruit in old age; they shall be fat / and flourishing; To shew … that the LORD *is* upright: *he is* / my rock, and *there is* no / unrighteousness in him.

93   **Psalm 93**

The LORD reigneth, he is clothed with / majesty; the LORD is / clothed with strength, *wherewith* he hath gir-ded himself: *and* the world … also is stablished, that it can-not be moved. Thy throne *is* / established of old: thou *art* from / everlasting. The floods … have lifted up, O LORD, the floods / have lifted up their voice; / the floods lift up their waves. The LORD / on high *is* mightier … than the noise of many waters, / *yea, than* the mighty waves / of the sea. Thy testimonies / are very sure: holi-ness becometh thine house, O LORD, / for ever.

94   **Psalm 94**

O LORD God, to whom vengeance be-longeth; O God, to whom / vengeance belongeth, shew thyself. / Lift up thyself, thou judge … of the earth: render a reward / to the proud. LORD, how long / shall the wicked, how long shall the / wicked triumph? *How long* … shall they utter *and* speak hard things? / *and* all the workers of / iniquity boast themselves? They / break in piec's thy people, … O LORD, and afflict thine heri-tage. They slay the widow / and the stranger, and murder the / fatherless. Yet they say, … The LORD shall not see, neither shall / the God of Jacob re-gard *it*. Understand, ye brutish / among the people: and … *ye* fools, when will ye be wise? He / that planted the ear, shall / he not hear? he that formed the eye, / shall he not see? He that … chastiseth the heathen, shall not / he correct? he that tea-cheth man knowledge, *shall not he know*? / The LORD knoweth the thoughts … of man, that they *are* vanity. / Blessed *is* the man whom / thou chastenest, O LORD, and tea-chest him out of thy law; … That thou mayest give him rest from / the days of adversi-ty, until the pit be digged for the / wicked. For the LORD … will not cast off his people, nei-ther will he forsake his / inheritance. But judgment shall / return to righteousness: … and all the upright in heart shall / follow it. Who will rise / up for me against the evil-doers? *or* who will stand … up for me against the workers / of iniquity? Un-less the LORD *had been* my help, my / soul had almost dwelt in … silence. When I said, My foot slip-peth; thy mercy, O LORD, / held me up. In the multitude / of my thoughts within me … thy comforts delight my soul. Shall / the throne of iniqui-ty have fellowship with thee, which / frameth mischief by a … law? They gather themselves toge-ther against the soul of / the righteous, and condemn the in-nocent blood. But the LORD … is my defence; and my God *is* / the rock of my refuge. / And he shall bring upon them their / own iniquity, and … shall cut them off in their own wi-ckedness; *yea*, the LORD our / God shall cut them off.

95   Psalm 95

O come, let us sing unto the / LORD: let us make a joy-ful noise to the rock of our / salvation. Let us come … before his presence with thanksgi-ving, and make a joyful / noise unto him with psalms. For the / LORD *is* a great God, and … a great King above all gods. In / his hand *are* the deep pla-ces of the earth: the strength of the / hills *is* his also. The … sea *is* his, and he made it: and / his hands formed the dry *land*. / O come, let us worship and bow / down: let us kneel before … the LORD our maker. For he *is* / our God; and we *are* / the people of his pasture, and / the sheep of his hand. To … day if ye will hear his voice, Har-den not your heart, as in / the provocation, *and* as *in* / the day of temptation … in the wilderness: When your fa-thers tempted me, *and* proved / me, and saw my work. Forty years / long was I grieved with *this* … generation, and said, It *is* / a people that do err / in their heart, and they have not known / my ways: Unto whom I … sware in my wrath that they should not / enter into my rest.

96   Psalm 96

O sing unto the LORD a new / song: sing unto the LORD, / all the earth. Sing unto the LORD, / bless his name; shew forth his … salvation from day to day. De-clare his glory among / the heathen, his wonders among / all people. For the LORD … *is* great, and greatly to be praised: / he *is* to be feared a-bove all gods. For all the gods of / the nations *are* idols: … but the LORD made the heavens.

Ho-nour and majesty *are* / before him: strength and beauty *are* / in his sanctuary. … Give unto the LORD, O ye kind-reds of the people, give / unto the LORD glory and strength. / Give unto the LORD the … glory *due unto* his name: bring / an offering, and come / into his courts. O worship the / LORD in the beauty of … holiness: fear before him, all / the earth. Say among the / heathen *that* the LORD reigneth: *and* / the world also shall be … established that it shall not be / moved: he shall judge the peo-ple righteously. Let the heavens / rejoice, and let the earth … be glad; let the sea roar, and the / fulness thereof. Let the / field be joyful, and all that *is* / therein: then shall all the … trees of the wood rejoice Before / the LORD: for he cometh, / for he cometh to judge the earth: / he shall judge the world with … righteousness, and the people with / his truth.

97   **Psalm 97**

The LORD reigneth; let the earth re-joice; let the multitude / of isles be glad *thereof.* Clouds and / darkness *are* round about … him: righteousness and judgment *are* / the habitation of / his throne. A fire goeth be-fore him, and burneth up … his enemies round about. His / lightnings enlightened the / world: the earth saw, and trembled. The / hills melted like wax at … the presence of the LORD, at the / presence of the Lord of / the whole earth. The heavens declare / his righteousness, and all … the people see his glory. Con-founded be all they that / serve graven images, *they* that / boast themselves of idols: … worship him, all *ye* gods. Zion / heard, and was glad; and the / daughters of Judah rejoiced be-cause of thy judgments, O … LORD. For thou, LORD, *art* high above / all the earth: thou art e-xalted far 'bove all gods. Ye that / love the LORD, hate evil: … he preserveth the souls of his / saints; he delivereth / them out of the hand of the wi-cked. Light is sown for the … righteous, and gladness for the up-right in heart. Rejoice in / the LORD, ye righteous; and give thanks / at the remembrance of … his holiness.

98   Psalm 98

According to Psalm *98.*

O sing unto the LORD a new / song; for he hath done mar-vellous things: his right hand, and his / holy arm, hath gotten … him the victory. The LORD hath / made known his salvation: / his righteousness hath he open-ly shewed in the sight of … the heathen. He hath remembered / his mercy and his truth / toward the house of Israel: / all the ends of the earth … have seen the salvation of our / God. Make a joyful noise / unto the LORD, all the earth: make / a loud noise, and rejoice, … and sing praise. Sing unto the LORD / with the harp; with the harp, / and the voice of a psalm. With trum-pets and sound of cornet … make a joyful noise before the / LORD, the King. Let the sea / roar, and the fulness thereof; the / world, and they that dwell there. … Let the floods clap *their* hands: let the / hills be joyful toge-ther Before the LORD; for he co-meth to judge the earth: with … righteousness shall he judge the world, / and the people with e-quity.

99   Psalm 99

The LORD reigneth; let the people / tremble: he sitteth *be-tween* the cherubims; let the earth / be moved. The LORD *is* great … in Zion; and he *is* high a-bove all the people. Let / them praise thy great and terrible / name; *for* it *is* holy. … The king's strength also loveth judg-ment; thou dost establish / equity, thou executest / judgment and righteousness … in Jacob. Exalt ye the LORD / our God, and worship *ye* / at his footstool; *for* he *is* ho-ly. Moses and Aaron … among his priests, and Samuel / among them that call u-pon his name; they called upon the / LORD, and he answered them. … He spake unto them in the clou-dy pillar: they kept his / testimonies, and the ordi-nance *that* he gave them. Thou … answeredst them, O LORD our God: / thou wast a God that for-gavest them, though thou tookest ven-geance of their inventions. ... Exalt the LORD our God, and wor-ship at his holy hill; / for the LORD our God *is* holy.

100   Psalm 100

According to a Psalm of praise.

Make a joyful noise unto the / LORD, all ye lands. Serve the / LORD with gladness: come before his / presence with singing. Know ... ye that the LORD he *is* God: *it* / *is* he *that* hath made us, / and not we ourselves; *we are* / his people, and the sheep ... of his pasture. Enter into / his gates with thanksgiving, / *and* into his courts with praise: be / thankful unto him, *and* ... bless his name. For the LORD *is* good; / his mercy *is* ever-lasting; and his truth *endureth* / to all generations.

101   Psalm 101

According to the Psalm of David.

I will sing of mercy and judg-ment: unto thee, O LORD, / will I sing. *And* I will behave / myself wisely in a ... perfect way. O when wilt thou come / unto me? I will walk / within my house with a perfect / heart. I will set no wick'd ... thing before mine eyes: I hate the / work of them that turn a-side; *it* shall not cleave to me. A / froward heart shall depart ... from me: I will not know a wi-cked *person.* Whoso pri-vily slandereth his neighbour, / him will I cut off: him ... that hath an high look and a proud / heart will not I suffer. / Mine eyes *shall be* upon the faith-ful of the land, that they ... may dwell with me: he that walketh / in a perfect way, he / shall serve me. He that worketh de-ceit shall not dwell within ... my house: he that telleth lies shall / not tarry in my sight. / I will early destroy all the / wicked of the land; that ... I may cut off all wicked do-ers from the city of / the LORD.

According to a Prayer of the afflicted, when he is overwhelmed, and poureth out his complaint before the LORD.

Hear my prayer, O LORD, and let / my cry come unto thee. / Hide not thy face from me in the / day *when* I'm in trouble; … incline thine ear unto me: in / the day *when* I call an-swer me speedily. For my days / are consumed like smoke, and … my bones are burned as an hearth. My / heart is smitten, and wi-thered like grass; so that I forget / to eat my bread. *And* by … reason of the voice of my groa-ning my bones cleave to my / skin. I am like a pelican / of the wilderness: I … am like an owl of the desert. / I watch, and am as a / sparrow alone upon the house / top. *And* mine enemies … reproach me all the day; *and* they / that are mad against me / are sworn against me. For I have / eaten ashes like bread, … and mingled my drink with weeping, / Because of thine indi-gnation and thy wrath: for thou hast / lifted me up, and cast … me down. My days *are* like a sha-dow that declineth; and / I am withered like grass. But thou, / O LORD, shalt endure for … ever; and thy remembrance un-to all generations. / Thou shalt arise, *and* have mercy / upon Zion: for the … time to favour her, yea, the set / time, is come. For thy ser-vants take pleasure in her stones, and / favour the dust thereof. … So the heathen shall fear the name / of the LORD, and all the / kings of the earth thy glory. When / the LORD shall build *it* up. … When *he* shall build up Zion, he / shall appear in his glo-ry. He will regard the prayer / of the destitute, and … not despise their prayer. This shall / be written for the ge-neration to come: and the peo-ple which shall be creat'd … shall praise the LORD. For he hath looked / down from the height of his / sanctuary; from heaven did / the LORD behold the earth; … To hear the groaning of the pri-soner; to loose those that / are appointed to death; To de-clare the name of the LORD … in Zion, and his praise in Je-rusalem; When the peo-ple are gathered together, and / the kingdoms, to serve the … LORD. He weakened my strength in the / way; he shortened my days. / I said, O my God, take me not / away in the midst of … my days: thy years *are* throughout all / generations. Of old / hast thou laid the foundation of / the earth: and the heavens … *are* the work of thy hands. They shall / perish, but thou shalt en-dure: yea, all of them shall wax old / like a garment; as a … vesture shalt thou change them, and they / shall be changed: But thou *art* / the same, and thy years shall have no / end. The children of thy … servants shall continue, and their / seed shall be established / before thee.

103   **Psalm 103**

According to the Psalm of David.

Bless the LORD, O my soul: and all / that is within me, *bless* / his holy name. Bless the LORD, O / my soul, and forget not … all his benefits: Who forgi-veth all thine iniqui-ties; who healeth all thy disea-ses; Who redeemeth thy … life from destruction; who crowneth / thee with lovingkindness / and tender mercies; Who satis-fieth thy mouth with good … *things; so that* thy youth is renewed / like the eagle's. The LORD / executeth righteousness and / judgment for all that are … oppressed. He made known his ways un-to Moses, his acts un-to the children of Israel. / The LORD *is* merciful … and gracious, slow to anger, and / plenteous in mercy. *And* / he will not always chide: neither / will he keep *his anger* … for ever. He hath not dealt with / us after our sins; / nor rewarded us according / to our iniquities. … For as the heaven is high a-bove the earth, *so* great is / his mercy toward them that fear / him. As far as the east … is from the west, *so* far hath he / removed our transgressions / from us. Like as a father pi-tieth *his* children, *so* … the LORD pitieth them that fear / him. For he knoweth our / frame; he remembereth that we / *are* dust. *As for* man, his … days *are* as grass: as a flower / of the field, so he flou-risheth. For the wind passeth o-ver it, and it is gone; … and the place thereof shall know it / no more. But the mercy / of the LORD *is* from everlas-ting to everlasting … upon them that fear him, and his / righteousness unto chil-dren's children; To such as keep his / covenant, and to those … that remember his commandments / to do them. The LORD hath / prepared his throne in the heavens; / and his kingdom ruleth … over all. Bless the LORD, ye his / angels, that excel in / strength, that do his commandments, hear-kening unto the voice … of his word. Bless ye the LORD, all / *ye* his hosts; *ye* mini-sters of his, that do his pleasure. / Bless the LORD, all his works … in all places of his domi-nion: bless the LORD, O my / soul.

104   Psalm 104

Bless the LORD, O my soul. O LORD / my God, thou art very / great; thou art clothed with honour and / majesty. Who cov'rest … *thyself* with light as *with* a gar-ment: who stretchest out the / heavens like a curtain: *And* who / layeth the beams of his … chambers in the waters: who ma-keth the clouds his chariot: / who walketh upon the wings of / the wind: Who maketh his … angels spirits; his ministers / a flaming fire: *Who* / laid the foundations of the earth, / *that* it should not be moved … for ever. Thou coveredst it / with the deep as *with* a / garment: the waters stood above / the mountains. *And* at thy … rebuke they fled; at the voice of / thy thunder they hasted / away. They go up by the moun-tains; they go down by the … valleys unto the place which thou / hast founded for them. Thou / hast set a bound that they may not / pass over; that they turn … not again to cover the earth. / He sendeth the springs in-to the valleys, *which* run among / the hills. They give drink to … every beast of the field: the wild / asses quench their thirst. By / them shall the fowls of the heaven / have their habitation, … *which* sing among the branches. He / watereth the hills from / his chambers: the earth is satis-fied with the fruit of thy … works. He causeth the grass to grow / for the cattle, and herb / for the service of man: that he / may bring forth food out of … the earth; And wine *that* maketh glad / the heart of man, *and* oil / to make *his* face to shine, and bread / *which* strengtheneth man's heart. … The trees of the LORD are full *of / sap*; the cedars of Le-banon, which he hath planted; Where / the birds make their nests: *as ... for* the stork, the fir trees *are* her / house. The high hills *are* a / refuge for the wild goats; *and* the / rocks for the conies. He ... appointed the moon for seasons: / the sun know'th his going / down. Thou makest darkness, and it / is night: wherein all the ... beasts of the forest do creep *forth.* / The young lions roar af-ter their prey, and seek their meat from / God. The sun ariseth, ... they gather themselves together, / and lay them down in their / dens. Man goeth forth unto his / work and to his labour ... until the evening. O LORD, / how manifold are thy / works! in wisdom hast thou made them / all: the earth is full of ... thy riches. *So is* this great and / wide sea, wherein *are* things / creeping innum'rable, both small / and great beasts. There go the ... ships: *there is* that leviathan, / *whom* thou hast made to play / therein. These wait all upon thee; / that thou mayest give *them* ... their meat in due season. *That* thou / givest them they gather: / thou openest thine hand, they are / filled with good. Thou hidest ... thy face, they are troubled: thou ta-kest away their breath, they / die, and return to their dust. Thou / sendest forth thy spirit, ... they are created: and thou re-newest the face of the / earth. The glory of the LORD shall / endure for ever: the ... LORD shall rejoice in his works. He / looketh on the earth, and / it trembleth: he toucheth the hills, / and they smoke. I will sing ... unto the LORD as long as I / live: I will sing praise to / my God while I have my being. / My meditation of ... him shall be sweet: I will be glad / in the LORD. Let the sin-ners be consumed out of the earth, / and let the wicked be ... no more. Bless thou the LORD, O my / soul. Praise ye the LORD.

105   Psalm 105

O give thanks unto the LORD; call / upon his name: make known / his deeds among the people. Sing / unto him, sing psalms to ... him: talk ye of all his wondrous / works. Glory ye in his / holy name: let the heart of them / rejoice that seek the LORD. ... Seek the LORD, and his strength: seek his / face evermore. Remem-ber his marvellous works that he / hath done; his wonders, and … the judgments of his mouth; O ye / seed of Abraham his / servant, ye children of Jacob / his chosen. He *is* the … LORD our God: his judgments *are* / in all the earth. He hath / remembered his covenant for / ever, the word *which* he … commanded to a thousand ge-nerations. Which *cov'nant* / he made with Abraham, and his / oath unto Isaac; … And confirmed the same unto Ja-cob for a law, *and* to / Israel *for* an everlas-ting covenant: Saying, … Unto thee will I give the land / of Canaan, the lot / of your inheritance: When they / were *but* a few men in … number; yea, very few, and stran-gers in it. When they went / from one nation to another, / *and* from *one* kingdom to … another people; *And* he suf-fered no man to do them / wrong: yea, he reproved kings for their / sakes; *Saying*, Touch not mine … anointed, and do my prophets / no harm. Moreover he / called for a famine upon the / land: *and* he brake the whole … staff of bread. He sent a man be-fore them, *even* Joseph, / *who* was sold for a servant: Whose / feet they hurt with fetters: … he was laid in iron: Until / the time that his word came: / the word of the LORD tried him. *And* / the king sent and loosed him; … *even* the ruler of the peo-ple, and let him go free. / He made him lord of his house, ru-ler of all his substance: … To bind his princes at his plea-sure; and teach his sena-tors wisdom. Israel also / came into Egypt; and … Jacob sojourned in the land of / Ham. And he increased his / people greatly; and made them stron-ger than their enemies. … He turned their heart to hate his peo-ple, to deal subtilly / with his servants. He sent Moses / his servant; *and* Aaron … whom he had chosen. They shewed his / signs among them, and won-ders in the land of Ham. He sent / darkness, and made it dark; … and they rebelled not against his / word. He turned their waters / into blood, and slew their fish. *And* / their land brought forth frogs in … abundance, in the chambers of / their kings. He spake, and there / came divers sorts of flies, *and* lice / in all their coasts. He gave … them hail for rain, *and* flaming fire / in their land. He smote their / vines also and their fig trees; and / brake the trees of their coasts. … He spake, and the locusts came, and / caterpillers, and that / without number, And did eat up / all the herbs in their land, … and devoured the fruit of their / ground. He smote also all / the firstborn in their land, the chief / of all their strength. He brought … them forth also with silver and / gold: and *there was* not one / feeble *person* among their tribes. / Egypt was glad when they … departed: for the fear of them / fell upon them. He spread / a cloud for a covering; and / fire to give light in … the night. *The people* asked, and he / brought quails, and satisfied / them with the bread of heaven. He / opened the rock, and the … waters *they* gushed out; *and* they ran / in the dry places *like* / a river. For he remembered / his holy promise, *and* … Abraham his servant. And he / brought forth his people with / joy, *and* his chosen with gladness: / And gave them the lands of … the heathen: and they inheri-ted the labour of the / people; That they might observe his / statutes, and keep his laws. … Praise ye the LORD.

106   **Psalm 106**

Praise ye the LORD. O give thanks to / the LORD; for *he is* good: / for his mercy *endureth* for / ever. Who can utter … the mighty acts of the LORD? *who* / can shew forth all his praise? / Bless'd *are* they that keep judgment, *and* / he that doth righteousness … at all times. Remember me, O / LORD, with the favour *that / thou bearest unto* thy people: / O visit me with thy … salvation; That I may see the / good of thy chosen, that / I may rejoice in the gladness / of thy nation, that I … may glory with thine inheri-tance. We have sinned with our / fathers, we have committed in-iquity, we have done / wickedly. Our fathers un-derstood not thy wonders / in Egypt; they remembered not / the multitude of thy … mercies; but provoked *him* at the / sea, *even* at the Red / sea. Nevertheless he saved them / for his name's sake, that he … might make his mighty power to / be known. He rebuked the / Red sea also, and it was dried / up: so he led them through … the depths, as through the wilderness. / And he saved them from the / hand of him that hated *them*, and / redeemed them from the hand … of the enemy. And the wa-ters covered their en'mies: / there was not one of them left. Then / believed they his words; they … sang his praise. They soon forgat his / works; they waited not for / his counsel: But lusted excee-dingly in the wild'ness, … and tempted God in the desert. / And he gave them their re-quest; but sent leanness into their / soul. They envied Moses … also in the camp, *and* Aaron / the saint of the LORD. The / earth opened and swallowed up Da-than, covered the comp'ny … of Abiram. And a fire / was kindled in their com-pany; the flame burned up the wi-cked. They made a calf in / Horeb, and worshipped the molten / image. Thus they changed their / glory into the simili-tude of an ox that eat'th … grass. They forgat God their saviour, / which had done great things in / Egypt; Wondrous works in the land / of Ham, *and* terrible … things by the Red sea. Therefore he / said that he would destroy / them, had not Moses his chosen / stood before him in the … breach, to turn away his wrath, lest / he should destroy *them*. Yea, / they despised the pleasant land, they / believed not his word: But … murmured in their tents, *and* hearkened / not unto the voice of / the LORD. Therefore he lifted up / his hand against them, to … overthrow them in the wilder-ness: To overthrow their / seed also among the nations, / and to scatter them in … the lands. They joined themselves also / unto Baal-peor, and / ate the sacrifices of the / dead. Thus they provoked *him* … to anger with their inventions: / and the plague brake in u-pon them. Then stood up Phinehas, / and *he* executed … judgment: and *so* the plague was stayed. / And that was counted un-to him for righteousness unto / all generations for … evermore. They angered *him* al-so at the waters of / strife, so that it went ill with Mo-ses for their sakes: Because … they provoked his spirit, so that / he spake unadvis'dly / with his lips. They did not destroy / the nations, concerning … whom the LORD commanded them: But / were mingled among the / heathen, and learned their works. And they / served their idols: which were … a snare unto them. Yea, they sa-crificed their sons and their / daughters unto devils, And shed / innocent blood, *even* … the blood of their sons and of their / daughters, whom they sacri-ficed unto the idols of Ca-naan: and the land was ... polluted with blood. Thus were they / defiled with their own works, / and went a whoring with their own / inventions. Therefore was ... the wrath of the LORD kindled a-gainst his people, inso-much that he abhorred his own in-heritance. And he gave ... them into the hand of the hea-then; and they that hated / them ruled over them. Their ene-mies also oppressed them, ... and they were brought into subjec-tion under their hand. Ma-ny times did he deliver them; / but they provoked *him* with ... their counsel, and were brought low for / their iniquity. Ne-vertheless he regarded their / affliction, when he heard ... their cry: He remembered for them / his covenant, and re-pented according to the mul-titude of his mercies. ... He made them also to be pi-tied of all those that car-ried them captives. Save us, O LORD / our God, and gather us ... from among the heathen, to give / thanks unto thy holy / name, *and* to triumph in thy praise. / Blessed *be* the LORD God ... of Israel from everlas-ting to everlasting: / and let all the people say, A-men. Praise ye the LORD.

107   **Psalm 107**

O give thanks unto the LORD, for / *he is* good: for his mer-cy *endureth* for ever. Let / the redeemed of the LORD ... say *so*, whom he hath redeemed from / the hand of the en'my; / And gathered them out of the lands, / from the east, and from the ... west, from the north, and from the south. / They wandered in the wil-derness in a solitary / way; they found no city ... to dwell in. Hungry and thirsty, / their soul fainted in them. / *And* then they cried unto the LORD / in their trouble, *and* he ... delivered them out of their dis-tresses. And he led them / forth by the right way, that they might / go to a city of ...habitation. Oh that *men* would / praise the LORD *for* his good-ness, and *for* his wonderful works / to the children of men! ... For he satisfieth the lon-ging soul, and filleth the / hungry soul with goodness. Such as / sit in darkness and in ... the shadow of death, *being* bound / in affliction and i-ron; Because they rebelled against / the words of God, and *they* ... contemned the counsel of the most /

High: Therefore he brought down / their heart with labour; they fell down, / and *there was* none to help. … Then they cried unto the LORD in / their trouble, *and* he saved / them out of their distresses. He / brought them out of darkness … and the shadow of death, and brake / their bands in sunder. Oh / that *men* would praise the LORD *for* his / goodness, and *for* his works … for his wonderful works to the / children of men! For he / hath broken the gates of brass, and / cut the bars of iron … in sunder. Fools because of their / transgression, and because / of their iniquities, are af-flicted. Their soul abhorr'th … all manner of meat; and they draw / near unto the gates of / death. Then they cry unto the LORD / in their trouble, *and* he … saveth them out of their distres-ses. He sent his word, and / healed them, and delivered *them* from / their destructions. Oh that … *men* would praise the LORD *for* his good-ness, and *for* his wonder-ful works to the children of men! / And let them sacrifice … the sacrifices of thanksgi-ving, and declare his works / with rejoicing. They that go down / to the sea in ships, that … do business in great waters; These / see the works of the LORD, / and his wonders in the deep. For / he commandeth, raiseth … the stormy wind, which lifteth up / the waves thereof. They mount / up to the heaven, they go down / again to the depths: their … soul is melted because of trou-ble. They reel to and fro, / and stagger like a drunken man, / and are at their wits' end. … Then they cry unto the LORD in / their trouble, and he brin-geth them out of their distresses. / He maketh the storm a … calm, so that the waves thereof are / still. Then are they glad be-cause they be quiet; so he brin-geth them to their desir'd … haven. Oh that *men* would praise the / LORD *for* his goodness, and / *for* his wonderful works to the / children of men! Let them … exalt him also in the con-gregation of the peo-ple, and praise him in the assem-bly of the elders. He … turneth rivers into a wil-derness, and the water-springs into dry ground; A fruitful / land into barrenness, … for the wickedness of them that / dwell therein. He turneth / the wilderness into a stan-ding water, and dry ground … into watersprings. And there he / maketh the hungry to / dwell, that they may prepare a ci-ty for habitation; ... And sow the fields, and plant vineyards, / which may yield fruits of in-crease. He blesseth them also, so / that they are multiplied ... greatly; and suffereth not their / cattle to decrease. A-gain, they are minished and brought low / through oppression, *and through* ... affliction, and sorrow. He pou-reth contempt upon prin-ces, and causeth them to wander / in the wilderness, *where ... there is* no way. Yet setteth he / the poor on high from af-fliction, and maketh *him* fami-lies like a flock. *And* the ... righteous shall see *it*, and rejoice: / and all iniquity / shall stop her mouth. Whoso *is* wise, / and will observe these *things*, ... even they shall understand the / lovingkindness of the / LORD.

108   **Psalm 108**

According to the Song *or* Psalm of David.

O God, my heart is fixed; I will / sing and give praise, even / with my glory. Awake, psalt'ry / and harp: I *myself* will ... awake early. I will praise thee, / O LORD, among the peo-ple: and I'll sing praises unto / thee among the nations. ... For thy mercy *is* great above / the heavens: and thy truth / *reacheth* unto the clouds. Be thou / exalted, O God, 'bove ... the heavens: and thy glory a-bove all the earth; That thy / beloved may be delivered: / save *with* thy right hand, and ... answer me. God hath spoken in / his holiness; I will / rejoice, I will divide Shechem, / and mete out the valley ... of Succoth. Gilead *is* mine; / Manasseh *is* mine; E-phraim also *is* the strength of / mine head; Judah *is* my ... lawgiver; Moab *is* my wash-pot; over Edom will / I cast out my shoe; ov'r Philis-tia will I triumph. ... Who will bring me into the strong / city? who will lead me / into Edom? *Wilt* not *thou*, O / God, *who* hast cast us off? ... and wilt not thou, O God, go forth / with our hosts? Give us / help from trouble: for vain *is* the / help of man. Through God we ... shall do valiantly: for he / *it is that* shall tread down / our enemies.

To the chief Musician, *According to the* Psalm of David.

Hold not thy peace, O God of my / praise; For the mouth of the / wicked and the mouth of the de-ceitful are opened 'gainst … me: they have spoken against me / with a lying tongue. They / compassed me about also with / words of hatred; and fought … against me without a cause. For / my love they are my ad-versaries: but I *give myself / unto* prayer. And they … have rewarded me evil for / good, and hatred for my / love. Set thou a wicked man o-ver him: and let Satan … stand at his right hand. When he shall / be judged, let him be con-demned: and let his prayer become / sin. Let his days be few; … *and* let another take his of-fice. Let his children be / fatherless, and his wife a wi-dow. Let his children be … continu'lly vagabonds, and / beg: *and* let them seek *their / bread* also out of their deso-late places. *And* let the … extortioner catch all that he / hath; and let the strangers / spoil his labour. Let there be none / to extend mercy to … him: neither let there be any / to favour his father-less children. Let his posteri-ty be cut off; *and then* … in the generation follo-wing let their name be blot-ted out. *And* let the iniqui-ty of his fathers be … remembered with the LORD; and let / not the sin of his mo-ther be blotted out. Let them be / before the LORD always, … that he may cut off the memo-ry of them from the earth. / Because that he remembered not / to shew mercy, but *he* … persecuted the poor and nee-dy man, that he might e-ven slay the broken in heart. As / he loved cursing, so let … it come unto him: as he de-lighted not in blessing, / so let it be far from him. *And* / as he clothed himself with … cursing like as with his garment, / so let it come into / his bow'ls like water, and like oil / into his bones. Let it … be unto him as the garment / *which* covereth him, and / for a girdle wherewith he is / girded continually. … *Let* this *be* the reward of mine / adversaries from the / LORD, and of them that speak evil / against my soul. But do … thou for me, O GOD the Lord, for / thy name's sake: because thy / mercy *is* good, deliver thou / me. For I *am* poor and … needy, and my heart is wounded / within me. I am gone / like the shadow when it decli-neth: I am tossed up and … down as the locust. My knees are / weak through fasting; and my / flesh faileth of fatness. I be-came also a reproach … unto them: *when* they looked on me / they shaked their heads. Help me, / O LORD my God: O save me ac-cording to thy mercy: … That they may know that this *is* thy / hand; *that* thou, LORD, hast done / it. Let them curse, but bless thou: when / they arise, let them be … ashamed; but let thy servant re-joice. Let mine adversa-ries be clothed with shame, and let them / cover themselves with their … own confusion, as with a man-tle. I'll greatly praise the / LORD with my mouth; yea, I'll praise him / among the multitude. … For he shall stand at the right hand / of the poor, to save *him* / from those that condemn his soul.

110   **Psalm 110**

According to the Psalm of David.

The LORD said unto my Lord, Sit / thou at my right hand, un-til I make thine enemies thy / footstool. The LORD shall send … the rod of thy strength out of Zi-on: rule thou in the midst / of thine enemies. Thy people / *shall be* willing in the … day of thy power, in the beau-ties of holiness from / the womb of the morning: thou hast / the dew of thy youth. The … LORD hath sworn, and will not repent, / Thou *art* a priest for ev'r / after the order of Melchi-zedek. The Lord at thy … right hand shall strike through kings in the / day of his wrath. He shall / judge among the heathen, he shall / fill *the places* with the … dead bodies; he shall wound the heads / over many countries. / He shall drink of the brook in the / way: therefore shall he lift … up the head.

111   Psalm 111

Praise ye the LORD. I will praise the / LORD with *my* whole heart, in / the assembly of the upright, / and *in* the congr'ation. ... The works of the LORD *are* great, sought / out of all them that have / pleasure therein. His work *is* ho-n'rable and glorious: ... and his righteousness, *it* endu-reth for ever. He hath / made his wonderful works to be / remembered: the LORD *is* ... gracious and full of compassion. / He hath given meat un-to them that fear him: he will e-ver be mindful of his ... covenant. He hath shewed his peo-ple the power of his / works, that he may give them the he-ritage of the heathen. ... The works of his hands *are* veri-ty and judgment; all his / commandments *are* sure. They stand fast / for ever and ever, ... *and are* done in truth and upright-ness. He sent redemption / unto his people: he hath com-manded his covenant ... for ever: holy and reve-rend *is* his name. The fear / of the LORD *is* the beginning / of wisdom: *and* a good ... understanding have all they that / do *his commandments*: his / praise endureth for ever.

112   Psalm 112

Praise ye the LORD. Bless'd *is* the man / *that* feareth the LORD, *that* / delighteth greatly in his com-mandments. His seed shall be ... mighty upon earth: the gene-ration of the upright / shall be bless'd. Wealth and riches *shall / be* in his house: and his ... righteousness endureth for e-ver. Unto the upright / there ariseth light in the dark-ness: *he is* gracious, and ... full of compassion, and righteous. / A good man sheweth fa-vour, and lendeth: he will guide his / affairs with discretion. ... Surely he shall not be moved for / ever: the righteous shall / be in everlasting remem-brance. He shall not be ' fraid ... of evil tidings: his heart is / fixed, trusting in the LORD. / His heart *is* established, he shall / not be afraid, until ... he see *his desire* upon / his enemies. He hath / dispersed, he hath given to the / poor; his righteousness *shall* ... endure for ever; his horn shall / be exalted with ho-nour. The wicked shall see *it*, and / be grieved; he shall gnash with ... his teeth, and melt away: the de-sire of the wicked / shall perish.

113   Psalm 113

Praise ye the LORD. Praise, O ye ser-vants of the LORD, praise the / name of the LORD. Blessed be the / name of the LORD from this ...time forth and for evermore. From / the rising of the sun / unto the going down of the / same the LORD'S name *is* to ... be praised. The LORD *is* high above / all nations, *and* his glo-ry above the heavens. Who *is* / like unto the LORD our ... God, who dwelleth on high, Who hum-bleth *himself* to behold / *the things that are* in heaven, and / in the earth! He raiseth ... up the poor out of the dust, *and* / lifteth the needy out / of the dunghill; That he may set / *him* with princes, *even* ... with the princes of his people. / He maketh the barren / woman to keep house, *and to be* / a joyful mother of ... children. Praise ye the LORD.

114   Psalm 114

When Israel went out of E-gypt, the house of Jacob / from a people of strange language; / Judah was his sanct'ry, ... *and* Israel his dominion. / The sea saw *it*, and fled: / Jordan was driven back. The moun-tains skipped like rams, *and* the ... little hills like lambs. What *ailed* thee, / O thou sea, that thou fledd'st? / thou Jordan, *that* thou wast driven / back? Ye mountains, *that* ye ... skipped like rams; *and* ye little hills, / like lambs? Tremble, thou earth, / at the presence of the Lord, at / the presence of the God ... of Jacob; Which turned the rock *in-to* a standing water, / the flint into a fountain of / waters.

Not unto us, O LORD, not un-to us, but unto thy / name give glory, for thy mercy, / for thy truth's sake. Wherefore … should the heathen say, Where *is* now / their God? But our God / *is* in the heavens: he hath done / whatsoever he hath … pleased. Their idols *are* silver and / gold, the work of men's hands. / They have mouths, but they speak not: eyes / have they, but they see not: … They have ears, but they hear not: no-ses have they, but they smell / not: They have hands, but they handle / not: feet have they, but they … walk not: neither speak they through their / throat. They that make them are / like unto them; *so is* ev'ry / one that trusteth in them. … O Israel, trust thou in the / LORD: he *is* their help and / their shield. O house of Aaron, trust / in the LORD: he *is* their … help and their shield. Ye that fear the / LORD, trust in the LORD: he / *is* their help and their shield. The LORD / hath been mindful of us: … he will bless *us*; he will bless the / house of Israel; he / will bless the house of Aaron. He / will bless them that fear the … LORD, *both* small and great. The LORD shall / increase you more and more, / you and your children. Ye *are* bless'd of / the LORD which made heav'n … and earth. The heaven, *even* the / heavens, *are* the LORD'S: but / the earth hath he given to the / children of men. The dead … praise not the LORD, neither any / that go down into si-lence. But we will bless the LORD from / this time forth and for ev'r. … Praise the LORD.

I love the LORD, because he hath / heard my voice *and* my sup-plications. Because he hath in-clined his ear unto me, … therefore will I call upon *him* / as long as I live. The / sorrows of death compassed me, and / the pains of hell gat hold … upon me: I found trouble and / sorrow. Then called I u-pon the name of the LORD; O LORD, / I beseech thee, deliv'r … my soul. Gracious *is* the LORD, and / righteous; yea, our God / *is* merciful. The LORD preser-veth the simple: I was … brought low, and he helped me. Return / unto thy rest, O my / soul; for the LORD hath dealt bounti-fully with thee. For thou … hast delivered my soul from death, / mine eyes from tears, *and* my / feet from falling. I will walk be-fore the LORD in the land … of the living. I believed, there-fore have I spoken: I / was greatly afflicted: I said / in my haste, All men *are* … liars. What shall I render un-to the LORD *for* all his / benefits toward me? I'll take / the cup of salvation, … and call upon the name of the / LORD. I will pay my vows / unto the LORD now in the pre-sence of all his people. … Precious in the sight of the LORD / *is* the death of his saints. / O LORD, truly I *am* thy ser-vant; I *am* thy servant, … *and* the son of thine handmaid: thou / hast loosed my bonds. I will / offer to thee the sacrifice / of thanksgiving, and will … call upon the name of the LORD. / I will pay my vows un-to the LORD now in the presence / of all his people, In … the courts of the LORD'S house, in the / midst of thee, O Jeru-salem. Praise ye the LORD.

117   **Psalm 117**

O praise the LORD, all ye nations: / praise him, all ye people. / For his merciful kindness is / great toward us: and the … truth of the LORD *endureth* for / ever. Praise ye the LORD.

118   **Psalm 118**

O give thanks unto the LORD; for / *he is* good: because his / mercy *endureth* for ever. / Let Israel now say, … that his mercy *endureth* for / ever. Let the house of / Aaron now say, that his mercy / *endureth* for ever. … Let them now that fear the LORD say, / that his mercy *endur'th* / for ever. I called upon the / LORD in distress: the LORD …answered me, *and set me* in a / large place. The LORD *is* on / my side; I will not fear: what can / man do unto me? The … LORD taketh my part with them that / help me: therefore shall I /

see *my desire* upon them / that hate me. *It's* better … to trust in the LORD than to put / confidence in man. *It's* / better to trust in the LORD than / to put confidence in … princes. All nations compassed me / about: but in the name / of the LORD will I destroy them. / They compassed me about; … yea, they compassed me about: but / in the name of the LORD / I will destroy them. They compassed / me about like bees; they … are quenched as the fire of thorns: / for in the name of the / LORD I will destroy them. Thou hast / thrust sore at me that I … might fall: but the LORD helped me. The / LORD *is* my strength and song, / and is become my salvation. / The voice of rejoicing … and salvation *is* in the ta-bernacles of the righteous: the right hand of the LORD do-eth valiantly. The … right hand of the LORD is exal-ted: the right hand of the / LORD doeth valiantly. I / shall not die, but live, and … declare the works of the LORD. The / LORD hath chastened me sore: / but he hath not given me o-ver unto death. Open … to me the gates of righteousness: / I will go into them, / *and* I will praise the LORD: This gate / of the LORD, in which the … righteous shall enter. I will praise / thee: for thou hast heard me, / and art become my salvation. / The stone *which* the builders … refused is become the head *stone* / of the corner. This is / the LORD'S doing; it *is* marvel-lous in our eyes. This *is* … the day *which* the LORD hath made; we / will rejoice and be glad / in it. Save now, I beseech thee, / O LORD: O LORD, I pray … thee, send now prosperity. Bless'd / *be* he that cometh in / the name of the LORD: we have blessed / you out of the house of … the LORD. God *is* the LORD, which hath / shewed us light: bind the sa-crifice with cords, *even* unto / the horns of the altar. … Thou *art* my God, and I will praise / thee: *thou art* my God, I / will exalt thee. O give thanks un-to the LORD; for *he is* … good: for his mercy *endureth* / for ever.

119 (1)   **Psalm 119**

Blessed *are* the undefiled in / the way, who walk in the / law of the LORD. Blessed *are* they / that keep his test'monies, … *and that* seek him with the whole heart. / They also do no i-niquity: they walk in his ways. / Thou hast commanded *us* ... to keep thy precepts diligen-tly. O that my ways were / directed to keep thy statutes! / Then shall I not be 'shamed, ... when I have respect unto all / thy commandments. I will / praise thee with uprightness of heart, / when I shall have learned thy ... righteous judgments. I will keep thy / statutes: O forsake me / not utterly. Wherewithal shall / a young man cleanse his way? ... by taking heed *thereto* accor-ding to thy word. With my / whole heart have I sought thee: O let / me not wander from thy ... commandments. Thy word have I hid / in mine heart, that I might / not sin against thee. Blessed *art* / thou, O LORD: teach me thy ... statutes. With my lips have I de-clared all the judgments of / thy mouth. I have rejoiced in the / way of thy test'monies, ... as *much as* in all riches. I / will meditate in thy / precepts, and have respect unto / thy ways. I will delight ... myself in thy statutes: I will / not forget thy word. Deal / bountifully with thy servant, / *that* I may live, and keep ... thy word. Open thou mine eyes, that / I may behold wondrous / things out of thy law. I *am* a / stranger in the earth: hide ... not thy commandments from me. My / soul breaketh for the lon-ging *that it hath* unto thy judg-ments at all times. Thou hast ... rebuked the proud *that are* cursed, / which do err from thy com-mandments. Remove from me reproach / and contempt; for I have ... kept thy testimonies. Princes / also did sit *and* speak / 'gainst me: *but* thy servant did me-ditate in thy statutes. ... Thy testimonies also *are* / my delight *and* my coun-sellers. My soul cleaveth unto / the dust: quicken thou me ... according to thy word. I have / declared my ways, and thou / heardest me: teach me thy statutes. / Make me to understand ... the way of thy precepts: so shall / I talk of thy wondrous / works. My soul melteth for heavi-ness: *O* strengthen thou me ... according unto thy word. Re-move from me the way of / lying: and grant me thy law gra-ciously. I have chosen ... the way of truth: thy judgments have / I laid *before me*. I / have stuck unto thy testimo-nies: O LORD, put me not ... to shame. I'll run the way of thy / commandments, when thou shalt / enlarge my heart. Teach me, O LORD, / the way of thy statutes; ... and I shall keep it *unto* the / end. Give me understan-ding, and I shall keep thy law; yea, / I shall observe it with … *my* whole heart. Make me to go in / the path of thy command-ments; for therein do I delight. / Incline my heart unto … thy testimonies, and not to / covetousness. Turn a-way mine eyes from beholding va-nity; *and* quicken thou … me in thy way. Stablish thy word / unto thy servant, who / *is devoted* to thy fear. Turn / away my reproach which … I fear: for thy judgments *are* good. / Behold, I have longed af-ter thy precepts: quicken me in / thy righteousness. Let thy … mercies come also unto me, / O LORD, *even* thy sal-vation, according to thy word. / So shall I have wherewith … to answer him that reproacheth / me: for I trust in thy / word. And take not the word of truth / utterly out of my … mouth; for I have hoped in thy judg-ments. So shall I keep thy / law continu'lly for ever / and ever. And I will … walk at liberty: for I seek / thy precepts. I will speak / of thy testimonies also / before kings, and will not … be ashamed. And I will delight / myself in thy command-ments, which I have loved. My hands al-so will I lift up to … thy commandments, which I have loved; / and I will meditate / in thy statutes. Remember the / word unto thy servant, … upon which thou hast caused me to / hope. This *is* my comfort / in my affliction: for thy word / hath quickened me. The proud … have had me greatly in deri-sion: *yet* have I not de-clined from thy law. I remembered / thy judgments of old, O … LORD; and have comforted myself. / Horror hath taken hold / upon me because of the wi-cked that forsake thy law. … Thy statutes have been my songs in / the house of my pilgri-mage. I have remembered thy name, / O LORD, in the night, and … have kept thy law. This I had, be-cause I kept thy precepts. / *Thou art* my portion, O LORD: I / have said that I would keep … thy words. I intreated thy fa-vour with *my* whole heart: be / merciful unto me accor-ding to thy word. I thought … on my ways, and turned my feet un-to thy testimonies. / I made haste, and delayed not to / keep thy commandments. The … bands of the wicked have robbed me: / *but* I have not forgot-ten thy law. At midnight I will / rise to give thanks unto … thee because of thy righteous judg-ments. I *am* a compa-nion of all *them* that fear thee, of / them that keep thy precepts. ... The earth, O LORD, is full of thy / mercy: teach me thy sta-tutes. Thou hast dealt well with thy ser-vant, O LORD, according ... unto thy word. Teach me good judg-ment and knowledge: for I / have believed thy commandments. Be-fore I was afflicted ... I went astray: but now have I / kept thy word. Thou *art* good, / and doest good; teach me thy sta-tutes. The proud have forged a ... lie against me: *but* I will keep / thy precepts with *my* whole / heart. Their heart is as fat as grease; / *but* I delight in thy ... law. *It is* good for me that I / have been afflicted; that / I might learn thy statutes. The law / of thy mouth *is* better ... unto me than thousands of gold / and silver. Thy hands have / made me and fashioned me: give me / understanding, that I ... may learn thy commandments. They that / fear thee will be glad when / they see me; because I have hoped / in thy word. I know, O ... LORD, that thy judgments *are* right, and / *that* thou in faithfulness / hast afflicted me. *And* let, I / pray thee, thy merciful ... kindness be for my comfort, ac-cording to thy word un-to thy servant. Let thy tender / mercies come unto me, ... that I may live: for thy law *is* / my delight. Let the proud / be ashamed; for they dealt perver-sely with me without a ... cause: *but* I will meditate in / thy precepts. Let those that / fear thee turn to me, and those that / have known thy test'monies. ... Let my heart be sound in thy sta-tutes; that I be not a-shamed. My soul fainteth for thy sal-vation: *but* I hope in ... thy word. Mine eyes fail for thy word, / saying, When wilt thou com-fort me? For I am become like / a bottle in the smoke; ... *yet* do I not forget thy sta-tutes. How many *are* the / days of thy servant? when wilt thou / execute judgment on ... them that persecute me? The proud / have digged pits for me, which / *are* not after thy law. All thy / commandments *are* faithful: ... they persecute me wrongfully; / help thou me. They had al-most consumed me on earth; but I / forsook not thy precepts. ... Quicken me after thy loving-kindness; so shall I keep / the testimony of thy mouth.

For ever, O LORD, thy word is / settled in heaven. Thy / faithfulness *is* unto all ge-nerations: *and* thou hast … established the earth, and it a-bideth. They continue / this day according to thine or-dinances: for all *are* … thy servants. Unless thy law *had / been* my delights, I should / then have perished in mine afflic-tion. I will nev'r forget … thy precepts: for with them thou hast / quickened me. I *am* thine, / save me; for I have sought thy pre-cepts. The wicked have wait'd … for me to destroy me: *but* I / will consider thy tes-timonies. I have seen an end / of all perfection: *but* … thy commandment *is* exceeding / broad. O how love I thy / law! it *is* my meditation / all the day. Thou through thy … commandments hast made me wiser / than mine enemies: for / they *are* ever with me. I have / more understanding than … all my teachers: for thy testi-monies *are* my medi-tation. I understand more than / the ancients, because I … keep thy precepts. I have refrained / my feet from every e-vil way, that I might keep thy word. / I have not departed … from thy judgments: for thou hast taught / me. How sweet are thy words / unto my taste! *yea, sweeter* than / honey to my mouth! Through … thy precepts I get understan-ding: therefore I hate e-very false way. Thy word *is* a lamp / unto my feet, and a … light unto my path. I have sworn, / and I will perform *it*, / that I will keep thy righteous judg-ments. I am afflicted … very much: quicken me, O LORD, / according unto thy / word. Accept, I beseech thee, the / freewill offerings of … my mouth, O LORD, and teach me thy / judgments. My soul *is* con-tinu'lly in my hand: yet do / I not forget thy law. … The wicked have laid a snare for / me: yet I erred not from / thy precepts. Thy testimonies / have I taken as an … heritage for ever: for they / *are* the rejoicing of / my heart. I have inclined mine heart / to perform thy statutes … alway, *even unto* the end. / I hate *vain* thoughts: but thy / law do I love. Thou *art* my hi-ding place and my shield: I … hope in thy word. Depart from me, / ye evildoers: for / I'll keep the commandments of my / God. Uphold me 'ccording … unto thy word, that I may live: / and let me not be a-shamed of my hope. Hold thou me up, / and I shall be safe: and ... I will have respect unto thy / statutes continu'lly. / Thou hast trodden down all them that / err from thy statutes: for ... their deceit *is* falsehood. Thou put-test away all the wi-cked of the earth *like* dross: therefore / I love thy test'monies. ... My flesh trembleth for fear of thee; / and I am afraid of / thy judgments. I have done judgment / and justice: leave me not ... to mine oppressors. Be surety / for thy servant for good: / *and* let not the proud oppress me. / Mine eyes fail for *this* thy ... salvation, and for the word of / thy righteousness. Deal with / thy servant according unto / thy mercy, and teach me ... thy statutes. I *am* thy servant; / give me understanding, / that I may know thy testimo-nies. *It is* time for *thee*, ... LORD, to work: *for* they have made void / thy law. Therefore I love / thy commandments above gold; yea, / above fine gold. Therefore ... I esteem all *thy* precepts *con-cerning* all *things to be* / right; *and* I hate every false way. / Thy testimonies *are* ... wonderful: therefore doth my soul / keep them. The entrance of / thy words giveth light; it giveth / understanding unto ... the simple. I opened my mouth, / and panted: for I longed / for thy commandments. Look thou on / me, and be merciful ... unto me, as thou usest to / do unto those that love / thy name. Order my steps in thy / word: and let not any ... iniquity have dominion / ov'r me. Deliver me / from the oppression of man: so / will I keep thy precepts. ... Make thy face to shine upon thy / servant; and teach me thy / statutes. Rivers of waters run / down mine eyes, because they ... keep not thy law. Righteous *art* thou, / O LORD, and upright *are* / thy judgments. Thy testimonies / *that* thou hast commanded ... *are* righteous and very faithful. / My zeal hath consumed me, / because mine enemies have for-gotten thy words. Thy word ... *is* very pure: therefore thy ser-vant loveth it. I *am* / small and despised: *yet* do not I / forget thy precepts. Thy ... righteousness *is* an everlas-ting righteousness, and thy / law *is* the truth. Trouble and an-guish have taken hold on ... me: *yet* thy commandments *are* my / delights. The righteousness / of thy testimonies *is* e-verlasting: *O* give me ... understanding, and I shall live. / I cried with *my* whole heart; / hear me, O LORD: I will keep thy / statutes. I cried unto … thee; save me, and I shall keep thy / testimonies. I pre-vented the dawning of the mor-ning, and cried: I hoped in … thy word. Mine eyes prevent the *night* / watches, that I might me-ditate in thy word. Hear my voice / according unto thy … lovingkindness: O LORD, quicken / me according to thy / judgment. They draw nigh that follow / after mischief: they are … far from thy law. Thou *art* near, O / LORD; and all thy command-ments *are* truth. Concerning thy tes-timonies, I have known … of old that thou hast founded them / for ever. Consider / mine affliction, and deliver / me: for I don't forget … thy law. Plead my cause, and deli-ver me: quicken me ac-cording to thy word. Salvation / *is* far from the wicked: … for they seek not thy statutes. Great / *are* thy tender mercies, / O LORD: quicken me according / to thy judgments. Many … *are* my persecutors and mine / enemies; *yet* do I / not decline from thy testimo-nies. *And* I beheld the … transgressors, and *I* was grieved; be-cause they kept not thy word. / Consider how I love thy pre-cepts: quicken me, O LORD, … according to thy lovingkind-ness. Thy word *is* true *from* / the beginning: and every one / of thy righteous judgments … *endureth* for ever. Princes / have persecuted me / without a cause: but my heart stan-deth in awe of thy word. … I rejoice at thy word, as one / that findeth great spoil. I / hate and abhor lying: *but* thy / law do I love. Seven … times a day do I praise thee be-cause of thy righteous judg-ments. Great peace have they which love thy / law: nothing shall offend … them. LORD, I have hoped for thy sal-vation, and done thy com-mandments. My soul hath kept thy tes-timonies; and I love … them exceedingly. I have kept / thy precepts and thy tes-timonies: for all my ways *are* / before thee. Let my cry … come near before thee, O LORD: give / me understanding ac-cording to thy word. Let my sup-plication come before … thee: deliver me according / to thy word. My lips shall / utter praise, when thou hast taught me / thy statutes. My tongue shall … speak of thy word: for all thy com-mandments *are* righteousness. / Let thine hand help me; for I have / chosen thy precepts. I … have longed for thy salvation, O / LORD; and thy law *is* my / delight. Let my soul live, and it /

shall praise thee; and let thy …judgments help me. I have gone a-stray like a lost sheep; seek / thy servant; for I do not for-get thy commandments.

120   **Psalm 120**

A Song of degrees.

In my distress I cried unto / the LORD, and he heard me. / Deliver my soul, O LORD, from / lying lips, *and* from a … deceitful tongue. What shall be gi-ven unto thee? or what / shall be done unto thee, thou false / tongue? Sharp arrows of the … mighty, with coals of juniper. / Woe is me, that I so-journ in Mesech, *that* I dwell in / the tents of Kedar! My … soul hath long dwelt with him that ha-teth peace. I *am for* peace: / but when I speak, they *are* for war.

121   **Psalm 121**

A Song of degrees.

I will lift up mine eyes unto / the hills, from whence cometh / my help. My help *cometh* from the / LORD, which made heaven and … earth. He will not suffer thy foot / to be moved: he that kee-peth thee will not slumber. Behold, / he that keepeth Isr'el … shall neither slumber nor sleep. The / LORD *is* thy keeper: the / LORD *is* thy shade upon thy right / hand. The sun shall not smite … thee by day, nor the moon by night. / The LORD shall preserve thee / from all evil: he shall preserve / thy soul. *And* the LORD shall … preserve thy going out and thy / coming in from this time / forth, and even for evermore.

122   Psalm 122

According to the Song of degrees of David.

I was glad when they said unto / me, Let us go into / the house of the LORD. Our feet / shall stand within thy gates, … O Jerusalem. Jerusa-lem is builded as a / city that is compact toge-ther: Whither the tribes go … up, the tribes of the LORD, unto / the testimony of / Israel, to give thanks unto / the name of the LORD. For … there are set thrones of judgment, the / thrones of the house of Da-vid. Pray for the peace of Jeru-salem: they shall prosper … that love thee. Peace be within thy / walls, *and* prosperity / within thy palaces. For my / brethren and companions' … sakes, I will now say, Peace *be* with-in thee. Because of the / house of the LORD our God I will / seek thy good.

123   Psalm 123

A Song of degrees.

Unto thee lift I up mine eyes, / O thou that dwellest in / the heavens. Behold, as the eyes / of servants *look* unto … the hand of their masters, *and* as / the eyes of a maiden / unto the hand of her mistress; / so our eyes *wait* on … the LORD our God, until that he / have mercy upon us. / Have mercy upon us, O LORD, / have mercy upon us: … for we are exceedingly filled / with contempt. Our soul / is exceedingly filled with the / scorning of those that are … at ease, *and* with the contempt of / the proud.

124   Psalm 124

According to the Song of degrees of David.

If *it had* not *been* the LORD who / was on our side, now / may Israel say; If *it had* / not *been* the LORD who was … on our side, when men rose up / against us: Then they had / swallowed us up quick, when their wrath / was kindled against us: … Then the waters had overwhelmed / us, the stream had gone o-ver our soul: Then the proud wa-ters had gone over our … soul. Blessed *be* the LORD, who hath / not given us *as* a / prey to their teeth. Our soul is / escaped as a bird out … of the snare of the fowlers: the / snare is broken, and we / are escaped. Our help *is* in / the name of the LORD, who … made heaven and earth.

125   Psalm 125

A Song of degrees.

They that trust in the LORD *shall be* / as mount Zion, *which* can't / be removed, *but* abideth for / ever. *As* the mountains … *are* round about Jerusalem, / so the LORD *is* round a-bout his people from henceforth e-ven for ever. For the … rod of the wicked shall not rest / upon the lot of the / righteous; lest the righteous put forth / their hands to in'quity. … Do good, O LORD, unto *those that* / *be* good, and to *them that* / *are* upright in their hearts. As for / such as turn aside to … their crooked ways, the LORD shall lead / them forth with the workers / of iniquity: *but* peace *shall* / *be* upon Israel.

126   Psalm 126

A Song of degrees.

When the LORD turned again the cap-tivity of Zion, / we were like them that dream. Then *there* / was our mouth filled with … laughter, and our tongue with sin-ging: then said they among / the heathen, The LORD hath done great / things for them. The LORD hath … done great things for us; *whereof* we / are glad. Turn again our / captivity, O LORD, as the / streams in the south. They that … sow in tears shall reap in joy. He / that goeth forth and wee-peth, bearing precious seed, shall *then* / doubtless come again with … rejoicing, bringing his sheaves *with / him.*

127   Psalm 127

According to the Song of degrees for Solomon.

Except the LORD build the house, they / labour in vain that build / it: except the LORD keep the ci-ty, the watchman waketh … *but* in vain. *It is* vain for you / to rise up early, to / sit up late, to eat the bread of / sorrows: *for* so he giv'th … his belov'd sleep. Lo, children *are* / an heritage of the / LORD: *and* the fruit of the womb *is / his* reward. As arrows … *are* in the hand of a mighty / man; so *are* children of / the youth. Happy *is* the man that / hath his quiver full of … them: they shall not be ashamed, but / they shall speak with the e-nemies in the gate.

128   Psalm 128

A Song of degrees.

Bless'd *is* every one that feareth / the LORD; that walketh in / his ways. For thou shalt eat the la-bour of thine hands: happy … *shalt* thou *be*, and *it shall be* well / with thee. Thy wife *shall be* / as a fruitful vine by the sides / of thine house: thy children ... like olive plants round about thy / table. Behold, that thus / shall the man be blessed that fea-reth the LORD. The LORD shall ... bless thee out of Zion: and thou / shalt see the good of Je-rusalem all the days of thy / life. Yea, thou shalt see thy ... children's children, *and* peace upon / Israel.

129   Psalm 129

A Song of degrees.

Many a time have they afflic-ted me from my youth, may / Israel now say: Many a / time have they afflicted ... me from my youth: yet they have not / prevailed against me. The / plowers plowed upon my back: they / made long their furrows. The ... LORD *is* righteous: he hath cut a-sunder the cords of the / wicked. Let them all be confoun-ded and turned back that hate ... Zion. Let them be as the grass / *upon* the housetops, which / withereth afore it groweth / up: Wherewith the mower ... filleth not his hand; nor he that / bindeth sheaves his bosom. / Neither do they which go by say, / The blessing of the LORD ... *be* upon you: we bless you in / the name of the LORD.

130   Psalm 130

A Song of degrees.

Out of the depths have I cried un-to thee, O LORD. Lord, hear / my voice: let thine ears be atten-tive to the voice of my ... supplications. If thou, LORD, shoul-dest mark iniquities, / O Lord, who shall stand? But *there is* / forgiveness with thee, that ... thou mayest be feared. I wait for / the LORD, my soul doth wait, / and in his word do I hope. My / soul *waiteth* for the Lord ... more than they that watch for the mor-ning: *I say, more than* they / that watch for the morning. Let Is-rael hope in the LORD: … for with the LORD *there is* mercy, / and with him *is* plenteous / redemption. And he shall redeem / Israel from all his … iniquities.

131   **Psalm 131**

According to the Song of degrees of David.

LORD, my heart is not haughty, nor / mine eyes lofty: neither / do I exercise myself in / great matters, or in things … too high for me. Surely I have / behaved and quieted / myself, as a child that is weaned / of his mother: my soul … *is* even as a weaned child. Let / Israel hope in the / LORD from henceforth and for ever.

132   **Psalm 132**

A Song of degrees.

LORD, remember David, *and* all / his afflictions: How he / sware unto the LORD, *and* vowed un-to the mighty *God* of … Jacob; Surely I will not come / into the taberna-cle of my house, nor go up in-to my bed; I will not … give sleep to mine eyes, *or* slumber / to mine eyelids, Until / I find out a place for the LORD, / an habitation for … the mighty *God* of Jacob. Lo, / we heard of it at Eph-ratah: we found it in the fields / of the wood. We will go … into his tabernacles: we / will worship at his foot-stool. Arise, O LORD, into thy / rest; thou, and the ark of … thy strength. Let thy priests be clothed with / righteousness; and let thy / saints shout for joy. For thy servant / David's sake turn not 'way … the face of thine anointed. The / LORD hath sworn *in* truth un-to David; he will not turn from / it; Of the fruit of thy … body will I set upon thy / throne. If thy children will / keep my covenant and my tes-timony that I shall … teach them, their children shall also / sit upon thy throne for

/ evermore. For the LORD hath cho-sen Zion; *and* he hath …
desired *it* for his habi-tation. This *is* my rest / for ever: here will I
dwell; for / I have desired it. … I will abundantly bless her /
provision: I will sa-tisfy her poor with bread. I will / also clothe her
priests with … salvation: and her saints shall shout / aloud for joy.
There will / I make the horn of David to / bud: I have ordained a …
lamp for mine anointed. His e-nemies will I clothe with / shame: but
upon himself shall his / crown flourish.

133   **Psalm 133**

According to the Song of degrees of David.

Behold, how good and how pleasant / *it is* for brethren to / dwell
together in unity! / *It is* like the precious … ointment upon the head,
that ran / down upon the beard, *e-ven* Aaron's beard: that went down
to / the skirts of his garments; … As the dew of Hermon, *and as /
the dew* that descended / upon the mountains of Zion: / for there the
LORD command'd … the blessing, *even* life for e-vermore.

134   **Psalm 134**

A Song of degrees.

Behold, bless ye the LORD, all *ye* / servants of the LORD, which /
by night stand in the house of the / LORD. Lift up your hands *in* …
the sanctuary, and bless the / LORD. The LORD that made hea-ven
and earth bless thee out of Zion.

135   **Psalm 135**

Praise ye the LORD. Praise ye the name / of the LORD; praise *him*,
O / ye servants of the LORD. Ye that / stand in the house of the …
LORD, in the courts of the house of / our God, Praise the LORD; /

for the LORD *is* good: sing praises / unto his name; for *it* ... *is* pleasant. For the LORD hath cho-sen Jacob unto him-self, *and* Israel for his pe-culiar treasure. For ... I know that the LORD *is* great, and / *that* our Lord *is* a-bove all gods. Whatsoever the / LORD pleas'd, *that* did he in ... heaven, and in earth, in the seas, / and all deep places. He / causeth the vapours to ascend / from the ends of the earth; ... he maketh lightnings for the rain; / he bringeth the wind out / of his treasuries. Who smote the / firstborn of Egypt, both ... of man and beast. *Who* sent tokens / and wonders into the / midst of thee, O Egypt, upon / Pharaoh, and upon ... all his servants. Who smote great na-tions, and slew mighty kings; / Sihon king of the Amorites, / and Og king of Bashan, ... and all the kingdoms of Canaan: / And gave their land *for* an / heritage, an heritage un-to Isr'el his people. ... Thy name, O LORD, *endureth* for / ever; thy memorial, / O LORD, throughout all genera-tions. For the LORD will judge ... his people, and he will repent / himself concerning his / servants. The idols of the hea-then *are* silver and gold, ... the work of men's hands. They have mouths, / but they speak not; eyes have / they, but they see not; They have ears, / but they hear not; neither ... is there *any* breath in their mouths. / They that make them are like / unto them: *so is* every one / that trusteth in them. Bless ... the LORD, O house of Israel: / bless the LORD, O house of / Aaron: Bless the LORD, O house of / Levi: ye that fear the ... LORD, bless the LORD. Blessed be the / LORD out of Zion, which / dwelleth at Jerusalem. Praise / ye the LORD.

136   Psalm 136

O give thanks unto the LORD; for / *he is* good: for his mer-cy *endureth* for ever. O / give thanks unto the God ... of gods: for his mercy *endu-reth* for ever. O give / thanks to the Lord of lords: for his / mercy *endur'th* for ev'r. ... To him who alone doeth great / wonders: for his mercy / *endureth* for ever. To him / that by wisdom made the ... heavens: for his mercy *endu-reth* for ever. To him / that stretch'd out the earth above the / waters: for his mercy ... *endureth* for ever. To him / that made great lights: for his / mercy *endureth* for ever: / The sun to rule by day: … for his mercy *endureth* for / ever: The moon and stars / to rule by night: for his mercy / *endureth* for ever. … To him that smote Egypt in their / firstborn: for his mercy / *endureth* for ever: And brought / out Israel from 'mong … them: for his mercy *endureth* / for ever: With a strong / hand, and with a stretched out arm: for / his mercy *endureth* … for ever. To him which divi-ded the Red sea into / parts: for his mercy *endureth* / for ever: And *who* made … Israel to pass through the midst / of it: for his mercy / *endureth* for ever: But o-verthrew Pharaoh and … his host in the Red sea: for his / mercy *endureth* for / ever. To him which led his peo-ple through the wilderness: … for his mercy *endureth* for / ever. To him which smote / great kings: for his mercy *endu-reth* for ever: And slew … famous kings: for his mercy *en-dureth* for ever: Si-hon king of the Amorites: for / his mercy *endureth* … for ever: And Og the king of / Bashan: for his mercy / *endureth* for ever: And gave / their land for an her'tage: … for his mercy *endureth* for / ever: *Even* an he-ritage unto Israel his / servant: for his mercy … *endureth* for ever. Who re-membered us in our low / estate: for his mercy *endu-reth* for ever: And hath … redeemed us from our enemies: / for his mercy *endu-reth* for ever. *And* who giveth / food to all flesh: for his … mercy *endureth* for ever. / O give thanks unto the / God of heaven: for his mercy / *endureth* for ever.

137   **Psalm 137**

By the rivers of Babylon, / there we sat down, yea, we / wept, when we remembered Zion. / We hanged our harps upon … the willows in the midst thereof. / For there they that carried / us away captive required / of us a song; and they … that wasted us *required of / us* mirth, *saying*, Sing us / *one* of the songs of Zion. How / shall we sing the LORD'S song … in a strange land? If I forget / thee, O Jerusalem, / let my right hand forget *her cun-ning. And* if I do not … remember thee, let my tongue cleave / to the roof of my mouth; / if I prefer not Jerusa-lem above my chief joy. … Remember, O LORD, the children / of Edom in the day / of Jerusalem; who said, Rase / *it*, rase *it, even* to … the foundation thereof. O daugh-ter of Babylon, who / art to be destroyed; happy *shall / he be*, that rewardeth … thee as thou hast served us. Happy / *shall he be*, that taketh / and dasheth thy little ones a-gainst the stones.

138   Psalm 138

According to the Psalm of David.

I will praise thee with my whole heart: / before the gods will I / sing praise unto thee. I will wor-ship toward thy holy … temple, and praise thy name for thy / lovingkindness and for / thy truth: for thou hast magnified / thy word above all thy … name. In the day when I cried thou / answeredst me, *and* strength-en'dst me *with* strength in my soul. All / the kings of the earth shall … praise thee, O LORD, when they hear the / words of thy mouth. Yea, they / shall sing in the ways of the LORD: / for great *is* the glory … of the LORD. Though the LORD *be* high, / yet hath he respect un-to the lowly: but the proud he / knoweth afar off. Though … I walk in the midst of trouble, / thou wilt revive me: thou / shalt stretch forth thine hand against the / wrath of mine enemies, … and thy right hand shall save me. The / LORD will perfect *that which* / concerneth me: thy mercy, O / LORD, *endureth* for ev'r: … forsake not the works of thine own / hands.

139   Psalm 139

To the chief Musician, *According to the* Psalm of David.

O LORD, thou hast searched me, and known / *me*. Thou knowest my down-sitting and mine uprising, thou / understandest my thought … afar off. Thou compassest my / path and my lying down, / and art acquainted *with* all my / ways. For *there is* not a … word in my tongue, *but*, lo, O LORD, / thou knowest it alto-gether. Thou hast beset me be-hind and before, and laid … thine hand upon me. *Such* knowledge / *is* too wonderful for / me; it is high, I cannot *at-tain* unto it. Whither … shall I go from thy spirit? or / whither shall I flee from / thy presence? If I ascend up / into heaven, thou *art* … there: if I make my bed in hell, / behold, thou *art there. If* / I take the wings of the morning, / dwell in the uttermost … parts of the sea; Even there shall / thy hand lead me, and thy / right hand shall hold me. If I say, / Surely the darkness shall … cover me; even the night shall / be light about me. Yea, / the darkness hideth not from thee; / but the night shineth as … the day: the darkness and the light / *are* both alike *to thee.* / For thou hast possessed my reins: thou / hast covered me in my … mother's womb. I will praise thee; for / I am fearfully *and* / wonderfully made: marvellous / *are* thy works; and *that* my … soul knoweth right well. My substance / was not hid from thee, when / I was made in secret, *and* cu-riously wrought in the … lowest parts of the earth. Thine eyes / did see my substance, yet / being unperfect; and in thy / book all *my members* were … written, *which* in continuance / were fashioned, when *as yet* / *there was* none of them. How precious / also are thy thoughts to … me, O God! how great is the sum / of them! *If* I should count / them, they are more in number than / the sand: when I awake, … I am still with thee. Surely thou / wilt slay the wicked, O / God: depart from me therefore, ye / bloody men. For they speak … against thee wickedly, *and* thine / enemies take *thy name* / in vain. Do not I hate them, O / LORD, that hate thee? and am … not I grieved with those that rise up / against thee? I hate them / with perfect hatred: I count them / mine enemies. Search me, … O God, and know my heart: try me, / and know my thoughts: And see / if *there be any* wicked way / in me, and lead me in … the way everlasting.

140   Psalm 140

To the chief Musician, *According to the* Psalm of David.

Deliver me, O LORD, from the / evil man: preserve me / from the violent man; Which i-magine mischiefs in *their* … heart; continu'lly are they ga-thered together *for* war. / They have sharpened their tongues like a / serpent; adders' poison … *is* under their lips. Interlude.
Keep me, O LORD, from the hands of / the wicked; preserve me / from the violent man; who have / purposed to overthrow … my goings. The proud have hid a / snare for me, and cords; they / have spread a net by the wayside; / they have set gins for me. Interlude.
I said unto the LORD, Thou *art* / my God: hear the voice of / my supplications, O LORD. O / GOD the Lord, the strength of … my salvation, thou hast covered / my head in the day of / battle. Grant not, O LORD, the de-sires of the wicked: … further not his wicked device; / *lest* they exalt themselves. Interlude.
As for the head of those that com-pass me about, let the / mischief of their own lips cover / them. Let burning coals fall … upon them: let them be cast in-to the fire; into / deep pits, that they rise not up a-gain. Let not an evil … speaker be established in the / earth: evil shall hunt the / violent man to overthrow / *him*. I know that the LORD … will maintain the cause of the af-flicted, *and* the right of / the poor. Surely the righteous shall / give thanks unto thy name: … the upright shall dwell in thy pre-sence.

141   Psalm 141

According to the Psalm of David.

LORD, I cry unto thee: make haste / unto me; give ear un-to my voice, when I cry unto / thee. Let my prayer be … set forth before thee *as* incense; / *and* the lifting up of / my hands *as* the evening sa-crifice. Set a watch, O … LORD, before my mouth; keep the door /

of my lips. Incline not / my heart to *any* evil thing, / to practise wicked works ... with men that work iniquity: / and let me not eat of / their dainties. Let the righteous smite / me; *and it shall be* a ... kindness: and let him reprove me; / *it shall be* an excel-lent oil, *which* shall not break my head: / for yet my pray'r also ... *shall be* in their calamities. / When their judges are o-verthrown in stony places, they / shall hear my words; for they ... are sweet. Our bones are scattered / at the grave's mouth, as when / one cutteth and cleaveth *wood* u-pon the earth. But mine eyes ... *are* unto thee, O GOD the Lord: / in thee is my trust; leave / not my soul destitute. Keep me / from the snares *which* they have ... laid for me, and the gins of the / workers of iniqui-ty. Let the wicked fall into / their own nets, whilst that I ... withal escape.

142   Psalm 142

According to the Maschil of David; A Prayer when he was in the cave.

I cried unto the LORD with my / voice; with my voice unto / the LORD did I make my suppli-cation. I poured out my ... complaint before him; I shewed be-fore him my trouble. When / my spirit was overwhelmed with-in me, then thou knewest ... my path. In the way wherein I / walked have they privily / laid a snare for me. I looked on / *my* right hand, and beheld, ... but *there was* no man that would know / me: refuge failed me; no / man cared for my soul. I cried un-to thee, O LORD: I said, ... Thou *art* my refuge *and* my por-tion in the land of the / living. Attend unto my cry; / for I am brought very ... low: deliver me from my per-secutors; for they are / stronger than I. Bring my soul out / of prison, that I may ... praise thy name: the righteous shall com-pass me about; for thou / shalt deal bountifully with me.

143   Psalm 143

According to the Psalm of David.

Hear my prayer, O LORD, give ear / to my supplications: / in thy faithfulness answer me, / *and* in thy righteousness. … And enter not into judgment / with *this* thy servant: for / in thy sight shall no man living / be justified. For the … enemy hath persecuted / my soul; he hath smitten / my life down to the ground; *and* he / hath made me to dwell in … darkness, as those that have been long / dead. Therefore is my spi-rit overwhelmed within me; *and* / my heart within me is … desolate. I remember the / days of old; I medi-tate on all thy works; I muse on / the work of thy hands. I … stretch forth my hands unto thee: my / soul *thirsteth* after thee, / as a thirsty land. Interlude.
Hear me speedily, O LORD: my / spirit faileth: hide not / thy face from me, lest I be like / unto them that go down … into the pit. Cause me to hear / thy lovingkindness in / the morning; for in thee do I / trust: cause me to know the … way wherein I should walk; for I / lift up my soul to thee. / Deliver me, O LORD, from mine / enemies: *for* I flee … to thee to hide me. Teach me to / do thy will; for thou *art* / my God: thy spirit *is* good; lead / me into the land of … uprightness. Quicken me, O LORD, / for thy name's sake: for thy / righteousness' sake bring my soul out / of trouble. And of thy … mercy cut off mine enemies, / and destroy all them that / afflict my soul: for I *am* thy / servant.

144   Psalm 144

According to the Psalm of David.

Blessed *be* the LORD my strength, which / teacheth my hands to war, / *and* my fingers to fight: My good-ness, and my fortress; my …high tower, and my deliv'rer; / my shield, and *he* in whom / I trust; who subdueth my peo-ple under me. LORD, what … *is* man, that thou takest knowledge / of him! *or* the son of / man, that thou makest account of / him! *For* man is like to … vanity: his days *are* as a / shadow that passeth a-way. Bow thy heavens, O LORD, and / come down: touch the mountains, … and they shall smoke. Cast forth lightning, / and scatter them: shoot out / thine arrows, and destroy them. Send / thine hand from above; rid … me, and deliver me out of / great waters, from the hand / of strange children; Whose mouth speaketh / vanity, and their right … hand *is* a right hand of falsehood. / I will sing a new song / unto thee, O God: on a psal-t'ry *and* an instrument … of ten strings will I sing praises / unto thee. *It is he* / that giveth salvation unto / kings: who delivereth … David his servant from the hurt-ful sword. Rid me, and de-liver me from the hand of strange / children, whose mouth speaketh … vanity, and their right hand *is* / a right hand of falsehood: / That our sons *may be* as plants / grown up in their youth; *that* … o'r daughters *may be* as corner / stones, polished *after* the / similitude of a palace: / *That* o'r garners *may be* … full, affording all manner of / store: *that* o'r sheep may bring / forth thousands and ten thousands in / our streets: *That* our … oxen *may be* strong to labour; / *that there be* no breaking / in, nor going out; that *there be* / no complaining in our … streets. Happy *is that* people, that / is in such a case: *yea*, / happy *is that* people, whose God / *is* the LORD.

145   **Psalm 145**

According to David's *Psalm* of praise.

I will extol thee, my God, O / king; and I will bless thy / name for ever and ever. E-v'ry day will I bless thee; … and I'll praise thy name for ever / and ever. Great *is* the / LORD, greatly to be praised; his great-ness *is* unsearchable. … One generation shall praise thy / works to another, and / shall declare thy mighty acts. I / will speak of the glorious … honour of thy majesty, and / of thy wondrous works. And / *men* shall speak of the might of thy / terrible acts: and I … will declare thy greatness. They shall / abundantly utter / the memory of thy great good-ness, and shall sing of thy … righteousness. The LORD *is* gracious, / and full of compassion; / slow to anger, and of great mer-cy. The LORD *is* good to … all: and his tender mercies *are* / over all his works. All / thy works shall praise thee, O LORD; and / thy saints shall bless thee. They … shall speak of the glory of thy / kingdom, and talk of thy / power; To make known to the sons / of men his mighty acts, … and the glorious majesty / of his kingdom. Thy king-dom *is* an everlasting king-dom, and thy dominion … *endureth* throughout all gene-rations. The LORD uphol-deth all that fall, and raiseth up / all *those that be* bowed down. … The eyes of all wait upon thee; / and thou givest them their / meat in due season. Thou open'st / thine hand, and satisfiest … the desire of every li-ving thing. The LORD *is* righ-teous in all his ways, and holy / in all his works. The LORD … *is* nigh unto all them that call / upon him, to all that / call upon him in truth. He will / fulfil the desire … of them that fear him: he also / will hear their cry, and will / save them. The LORD preserveth all / them that love him: but all … the wicked will he destroy. My / mouth shall speak the praise of / the LORD: and let all flesh bless his / holy name for ever … and ever.

146   Psalm 146

Praise ye the LORD. Praise the LORD, O / my soul. While I live will / I praise the LORD: I will sing prai-ses unto my God while … I have any being. Put not / your trust in princes, *nor* / in the son of man, in whom *there* / *is* no help. His breath go'th … forth, he returneth to his earth; / in that very day his / thoughts perish. Happy *is he* that / *hath* the God of Jacob … for his help, whose hope *is* in the / LORD his God: Which made hea-ven, and earth, the sea, and all that / therein *is*: which keepeth … truth for ever: Which execu-teth judgment for the op-pressed: which giveth food to the hun-gry. The LORD looseth the … prisoners: The LORD openeth / *the eyes of* the blind: the / LORD raiseth them that are bowed down: / the LORD lov'th the righteous: … The LORD preserveth the strangers; / he relieveth the fa-therless and widow: but the way / of the wicked he turn'th … upside down. The LORD shall reign for / ever, *even* thy God, / O Zion, unto all gene-rations. Praise ye the LORD.

147   **Psalm 147**

Praise ye the LORD: for *it is* good / to sing praises unto / our God; for *it is* pleasant; *and* / praise is comely. The LORD … doth build up Jerusalem: he / gathereth together / the outcasts of Israel. He / healeth the broken in … heart, and bindeth up their wounds. He / telleth the number of / the stars; he calleth them all by / *their* names. Great *is* our … Lord, and of great power: his un-derstanding *is* infi-nite. The LORD lifteth up the meek: / he casteth the wicked … down to the ground. Sing unto the / LORD with thanksgiving; sing / praise upon the harp unto o-ur God: Who covereth … the heaven with clouds, who prepa-reth rain for the earth, who / maketh grass to grow upon the / mountains. He giveth to … the beast his food, *and* to the young / ravens which cry. He de-lighteth not in the strength of the / horse: he tak'th not pleasure … in the legs of a man. The LORD / taketh pleasure in them / that fear him, in those that hope in / his mercy. Praise the LORD, … O Jerusalem; praise thy God, / O Zion. For he hath / strengthened the bars of thy gates; he / hath blessed thy children … within thee. He maketh peace *in* / thy borders, *and* filleth / thee with the finest of the wheat. / *And* he sendeth forth his … commandment *upon* earth: his word / runneth very swiftly. / He giveth snow like wool: he scat-tereth the hoarfrost like / ashes. He casteth forth his ice / like morsels: who can stand / before his cold? He sendeth out / his word, and melteth them: … he causeth his wind to blow, *and* / the waters flow. He shew-eth his word unto Jacob, his / statutes and his judgments … unto Israel. He hath not / dealt so with any na-tion: and *as for his* judgments, they / have not known them. Praise ye … the LORD.

148   Psalm 148

Praise ye the LORD. Praise ye the LORD / from the heavens: praise him / in the heights. Praise ye him, all his / angels: praise ye him, all … his hosts. Praise ye him, sun and moon: / praise him, all ye stars of / light. Praise him, ye heavens of hea-vens, and ye waters that … *be* above the heavens. Let them / praise the name of the LORD: / for he commanded, and they were / created. *And* he hath … also stablished them for ever / and ever: he hath made / a decree which shall not pass. Praise / the LORD from the earth, ye … dragons, and all deeps: Fire, and / hail; snow, and vapour; stor-my wind fulfilling his word: Moun-tains, and all hills; fruitful … trees, and all cedars: Beasts, and all / cattle; creeping things, and / flying fowl: Kings of the earth, and / all people; princes, and … all judges of the earth: Both young / men, and maidens; old men, / and children: Let them praise the name / of the LORD: for his name … alone is excellent; his glo-ry *is* above the earth / and heaven. He also exalt'th the horn / of his people, … the praise of all his saints; *even* / of the children of Is-rael, a people near unto / him. Praise ye the LORD.

149   Psalm 149

Praise ye the LORD. Sing unto the / LORD a new song, *and* his / praise in the congregation of / saints. Let Isr'el rejoice … in him that made him: let the chil-dren of Zion be joy-ful in their King. Let them praise his / name in the dance: let them … sing praises unto him with the / timbrel and harp. For the / LORD taketh pleasure in his peo-ple: he will beautify … the meek with salvation. Let the / saints be joyful in glo-ry: let them sing aloud upon / their beds. *Let* the high *prais's* …of God *be* in their mouth, and a / two edged sword in their / hand; To execute vengeance on / the heathen, punishments … upon the people; To bind their / kings with chains, and their no-bles with fetters of iron; To / execute upon them … the judgment written: this honour / have all his saints. Praise ye / the LORD.

150   **Psalm 150**

Praise ye the LORD. Praise God in his / sanctuary: praise him / in the firmament of his po-wer. Praise him for his might … for his mighty acts: praise him ac-cording to his excel-lent greatness. Praise him with the sound / of the trumpet: praise him … with the psalt'ry and harp. Praise him / with the timbrel and dance: / praise him with stringed instruments and / organs. Praise him upon … the loud cymbals: praise him upon / the high sounding cymbals. / Let every thing that hath breath praise / the LORD. Praise ye the LORD.

151   **Genesis 49:10**

O give thanks unto the LORD; call / upon his name: make known / his deeds among the people. Sing / unto him, sing psalms to … him: talk ye of all his wondrous / works. The sceptre did not / depart from Judah, nor a law-giver from between his … feet, until Shiloh came, Jesus / Christ; and unto him is / the gathering of the people. / Christ is the true Joseph … who was sold to Egypt for his / brothers, he proofeth us / as Joseph to see if we im-prove. He was cast into … the pit for us, but came out of / it. He died and rose a-gain. As Job suffered the inno-cent at the cross and his … friends mocked him. He is the angel / who went before them out / of Egypt, it was he that vi-sited Abraham in … the plains of Mamre and after-wards took Lot out of So-dom. Christ appeared to Moses out / of the bush and also … to Jakob at the ladder to / heaven. Isaiah saw / Christ sitting upon a throne, high / and lifted up, and his … train filled the temple. Ezeki-el saw the Lord on the / likeness of a throne in the like-ness as the appearance … of a man with brightness round a-bout. Joshua met Christ / at the entry of Canaan. / Now, the mountain of the … LORD'S house is established in the / top of the mountains, and / is exalted above the hills; / and all nations flow to … it. The hire of Tyre is / holiness to the LORD, / Ethiopia brings the present / unto the LORD of hosts. … Blessed is Egypt his people, / and Assyria is / the work of his hands. Israel / is the third with Egypt … and with Assyria, even / a blessing in the midst / of the land. And Ephraim doth / not envy Judah, and … Judah doth not vex Ephraim. / No one hurteth nor de-stroyeth in all my holy moun-tain: for the earth is full … of the knowledge of the LORD, as / the waters cover the / sea. There is a root of Jesse, / which standeth for a sign … of the people; and the rest of / Jesus Christ is glorious. / For unto us a child is born, / unto us a son is … given: and the government is / upon his shoulder: and / his name is called Wonderful, Coun-seller, The mighty God, … The everlasting Father, The / Prince of Peace. And of peace / there is no end, upon the throne / of David. The zeal of … the LORD of hosts doth perform this. / Praise ye the LORD.

152   The Ten Commandments

Moses went up unto God on / mount Sinai, and God / spake all these words, saying, I *am* / the LORD thy God, which have … brought thee out of the land of E-gypt, out of the house of / bondage. Thou shalt have no other / gods before me. Thou shalt … not make unto thee any gra-ven image, or any / likeness *of any thing* that *is* / in heaven above, or … that *is* in the earth beneath, or / that *is* in the water / under the earth: Thou shalt not bow / down thyself to them, nor … serve them: for I the LORD thy God / *am* a jealous God, vi-siting the iniquity of / the fathers upon the … children unto the third and fourth / *generation* of them / that hate me; And shewing mercy / unto thousands of them … that love me, and keep my command-ments. Thou shalt not take the / name of the LORD thy God in vain; / for the LORD will not hold … him guiltless that taketh his name / in vain. Remember the / sabbath day, to keep it holy. / Six days shalt thou labour, … and do all thy work: But the se-venth day *is* the sabbath / of the LORD thy God: *in it* thou / shalt not do any work,

... thou, nor thy son, nor thy daughter, / thy manservant, nor thy / maidservant, nor thy cattle, nor / thy stranger that *is* with ... within thy gates: For *in* six days / the LORD made heaven and / earth, and the sea, and all that in / them *is*, and rested the .... seventh day: wherefore the LORD blessed / the sabbath day, and hal-lowed it. Honour thy father and / thy mother: that thy days ... may be long upon the land which / the LORD thy God giveth / thee. Thou shalt not kill. Thou shalt not / commit adultery. ... Thou shalt not steal. Thou shalt not bear / false witness against thy / neighbour. Thou shalt not covet thy / neighbour's house, thou shalt not ... covet thy neighbour's wife, nor his / manservant, nor his maid-servant, nor his ox, nor his ass, / nor any thing that *is* ... thy neighbour's. The LORD gave Moses / two tables of testi-mony, tables of stone, written / with the finger of God.

153   **Exodus 29:7**

A Song of thanksgiving.

Thanks be to thee Father, Son and / Holy Spirit, that thou / hast consecrated us with oil / of holy ointment, with ... pure myrrh, sweet cinnamon, cal'mus / and cassia, and hast / sanctified all vessels of the / church. We thank thee that thou ... hearest our prayers as we of-fer our perfume: sta-cte, onycha, galbanum and / pure frankincense, pure *and* ... holy. Thou hast arrayed us in / fine linen, with good works / that thou doest through us. We thank / thee that we may bring half ... a shekel for the atonement / of our souls as thou / hast commanded Moses on the / mountain. We thank thee that ... Christ took the sicknesses of those / whom he healed and that all / may get the same reward whether / they came early or late ... to the vineyard. Thou art gracious / to all and a Saviour / of all men, specially of those / that believe, specially ... for the elect. For them, O Lord / Jesus Christ, thou took'st the / entire torment of hell and / only a part remains ... for us to suffer in this val-ley of Baca.

Receive / thou our offering as we / serve thee here now in the … New Testament! Blessed be the / name of the LORD from this / time forth and for evermore. A-men.

154   The Song of Moses / Deuteronomy 32

Give ear, O ye heavens, and I / will speak; and hear, O earth, / the words of my mouth. My doctrine / shall drop as the rain, my … speech shall distil as the dew, as / the small rain upon the / tender herb, and as the showers / upon the grass: Because … I will publish the name of the / LORD: ascribe ye greatness / unto our God. *He is* the Rock, / his work *is* perfect: for … all his ways *are* judgment: a God / of truth and without in-iquity, just and right *is* he. / They have corrupt'd themselves, … their spot *is* not *the spot* of his / children: *they are* a per-verse and crooked generation. / Do ye thus requite the … LORD, O foolish people and un-wise? *is* not he thy fa-ther *that* hath bought thee? hath he not / made thee, and established … thee? Remember the days of old, / consider the years of / many generations: ask thy / father, and he will shew … thee; thy elders, and they will tell / thee. When the most High di-vided to the nations their in-heritance, *and* when he … separated the sons of A-dam, he set the bounds of / the people according to the / number of the children … of Israel. For the LORD'S por-tion *is* his people; Ja-cob *is* the lot of his inhe-ritance. He found him in … a desert land, and in the waste / howling wilderness; he / led him about, he instructed / him, he kept him as the … apple of his eye. As an ea-gle stirreth up her nest, / fluttereth over her young, sprea-deth abroad her wings, tak'th … them, beareth them on her wings: *So* / the LORD alone did lead / him, and *there was* no strange god with / him. He made him ride on … the high places of the earth, that / he might eat the increase / of the fields; and he made him to / suck honey out of the … rock, and oil out of the flinty / rock; Butter of kine, and / milk of sheep, with fat of lambs, and / rams of the breed Bashan's, … and goats, with the fat of kidneys / of wheat; and thou didst drink / the pure blood of the grape. But Jesh-urun waxed fat, and kicked: … thou art waxen fat, thou art grown / thick, thou art covered *with / fatness*; then he forsook God *which* / made him, and lightly ‘ steemed … the Rock of his salvation. They / provoked him to jealou-sy with strange *gods*, with abomi-nations provoked they him … to anger. They sacrificed un-to devils, not to God; / to gods whom they knew not, to new / *gods that* came newly up, … whom your fathers feared not. Of the / Rock *that* begat thee thou / art unmindful, and hast forgot-ten God that formed thee. And … when the LORD saw *it*, he abhorred / *them*, because of the pro-voking of his sons, and of his / daughters. And he said, I … will hide my face from them, I will / see what their end *shall be*: / for they *are* a very froward / generation, children … in whom *is* no faith. They have moved / me to jealousy with / *that which is* not God; they have pro-voked me to anger with … their vanities: and I will move / them to jealousy with / *those which are* not a people; I’ll / provoke them to anger … with a foolish nation. For a / fire is kindled in / mine anger, and shall burn unto / the lowest hell, and shall … consume the earth with her increase, / and set on fire the / foundations of the mountains. I / will heap mischiefs upon … them; I will spend mine arrows u-pon them. *They shall be* burnt / with hunger, and devoured with / burning heat, with bitter … destruction: I’ll also send the / teeth of beasts upon them, / with the poison of serpents of / the dust. The sword without, … and terror within, shall destroy / both the young man and the / virgin, the suckling *also* with / the man of gray hairs. I … said, I would scatter them into / corners, I would make the / remembrance of them to cease from / among men: Were it not … that I feared the wrath of the e-nemy, lest their adver-saries should behave themselves stran-gely, lest they should say, Our … hand *is* high, and the LORD hath not / done all this. For they *are* / a nation void of counsel, nei-ther *is* in them *any* … understanding. O that they were / wise, *that* they understood / this, *that* they would consider their / latter end! How should one … chase a thousand, and two put ten / thousand to flight, except / their Rock had sold them, and the LORD / had shut them up? For their … rock *is* not as our Rock, e-ven our enemies / themselves *being* judges. For their / vine *is* of the vine of … Sodom, and of the fields of Go-morrah: their grapes *are* grapes / of gall, their clusters *are* bitter: / Their wine *is* the poison … of dragons, and the cruel ve-nom of asps. *Is* not this / laid up in store with me, *and* sealed / up among my treasures? … To me *belongeth* vengeance, and / recompence; their foot shall / slide in *due* time: for the day of / their calamity *is* … at hand, and the things that shall come / upon them make haste. For / the LORD shall judge his people, and / repent himself for his … servants, when he seeth that *their* / power is gone, and *there* / *is* none shut up, or left. And he / shall say, Where *are* their gods, … *their* rock in whom they trusted, Which / did eat the fat of their / sacrifices, *and* drank the wine / of their drink offerings? … let them rise up and help you, *and* / be your protection. See / now that I, *even* I, *am* he, / and *there is* no god with … me: I kill, and I make alive; / I wound, and I heal: nei-ther *is there any* that can de-liver out of my hand. … For I lift up my hand to hea-ven, and say, I live for / ever. If I whet my glitt'ring / sword, and mine hand take hold … on judgment; I will render ven-geance to mine enemies, / and will reward them that hate me. / I'll make mine arrows drunk … with blood, and my sword shall devour / flesh; *and that* with the blood / of the slain and of the captives, / from the beginning of … revenges upon the ene-my. Rejoice, O ye na-tions, *with* his people: for he will / avenge the blood of his … servants, and will render vengeance / to his adversaries, / and will be merciful unto / his land, to his people.

155   **Isaiah 2**

O sing unto the LORD a new / song; for the day of the / LORD of hosts shall be upon e-very one that is proud and … lofty, and upon every one / that is lifted up; and / he shall be brought low. And the lof-tiness of man shall be … bowed down, and the haughtiness of / men shall be made low: and / the LORD alone shall be exal-ted in that day. And the … idols he shall utterly a-bolish. And they shall go / into the holes of the rocks, and / into the caves of the … earth, for fear of the LORD, and for / the glory of his ma-jesty, when he ariseth to / shake terribly the earth. … Cease ye from man, whose breath is in / his nostrils: for wherein / is he to be accounted of? / The Lord hath washed away … the filth of the daughters of Zi-on, and hath purged the blood / of Jerusalem from the midst / thereof by the spirit … of judgment, and by the spirit / of burning. And the LORD / created upon every dwel-ling place of mount Zion … a cloud and smoke by day, and the / shining of a flaming / fire by night: for on all the / glory is a defence. … And there is a tabernacle / for a shadow in the / daytime from the heat, and for a / place of refuge, and for … a covert from storm and from rain. / Woe unto them that call / evil good, and good evil; that / put darkness for light, and … light for darkness; that put bitter / for sweet, and sweet for bit-ter! Woe unto them that are wise / in their own eyes, and are … prudent in their own sight! Woe un-to them that are mighty / to drink wine, and men of strength to / mingle strong drink: And which … justify the wicked for re-ward, and take away the / righteousness of the righteous from / him! Therefore as the fire … devoureth the stubble, and the / flame consumeth the chaff, / so their root shall be as rotten-ness, and their blossom shall … go up as dust: because they have / cast away the law of / the LORD of hosts, and despised the / word of the Holy One … of Israel. And he lifted / up an ensign to the / nations from far, and hissed unto / them from the end of the … earth. The desire of all na-tions is come. The heavens / and the earth were shaken and the / LORD made Zerubbabel … as a signet. The transgression / is finished, and there is / an end of sins, and everlas-ting righteousness is brought … in, and the vision and prophe-cy is sealed up, and the / most Holy is anointed.

Babylon is overthrown, the / Medes have destroyed it and / their name is cut off. Assyri-a is tread under foot … as the LORD of hosts hath sworn. He / hath destroyed the remnant / of the Philistines. Moab is / brought to silence and they … are cut off from being a na-tion. Edom is made per-petual desolations. And / the Ammonites are not … remembered. Tyrus is like the / top of a rock and a / place for the spreading of nets. And / Egypt remains a base … kingdom. Upon all the heathen / the judgment written was / executed. Praise ye the LORD.

157   Isaiah 58:13-14

A Song for the sabbath day.

Turn away thy foot from the sab-bath, from doing thy plea-sure on my holy day; and call / the sabbath a delight, … the holy of the LORD, honou-rable; honour him, do / not thine own ways, nor find thine own / pleasure, nor speake thine own … words: Then shalt thou delight thyself / in the LORD; and I will / cause thee to ride upon the high / places of the earth, and … feed thee with the heritage of / Jacob thy father: for / the mouth of the LORD hath spoken / it. What man shall there be … among you, that shall have one sheep, / and if it fall into / a pit on the sabbath day, will / he not lay hold on it, … and lift it out? Wherefore it is / lawful to do well on / the sabbath days, thus Christ taught and / healed the sick on sabbath. … The sabbath was made for man, and / not man for the sabbath. / The Son of man is Lord also / of the sabbath. And the … early church met at the first day / of the week, the day of / the Lord, the Sunday, on the day / on which he rose again … the disciples met to keep this / day holy. In the law / it is written, that on the sab-bath days the priests in the / temple profane the sabbath, and / are blameless. It is writ-ten that David, when he was an / hungred, and they that were … with him; they entered into the / house of God, and they did / eat the shewbread, which was not law-ful for them to eat, but … only for the priests. But God will / have mercy, and not sa-crifice.

158   Jonah

The word of the LORD commanded: / Jonah, to Nineveh! / Go, cry against that great city; / their wickedness is great. … Jonah fled by ship to Tarshish, / but the LORD sent a wind; / the mariners searched for the cause / and found it with Jonah. … And into the sea they cast him / there swallowed him a fish. / „In distress I cried to the Lord, / in the belly of hell, … yea, I am cast out of thy sight, / yet hast thou saved my life; / into thine temple came my pray'r, / to thee, O LORD my God. … They that observe wrong vanities, / forsake their own mercy. / But I will offer thanksgiving, / salvation is the LORD'S.“ … The word of the LORD came again: / Go unto Nineveh, / preach unto it that I bid thee. / Jonah arose, and went. … „Yet forty days for Nineveh / it shall be overthrown.“ / They believed and proclaimed a fast / as the King commanded. … And God did not do them evil, / but Jonah was angry, / saying: „Therefore I fled before / because thou art gracious. … It is better for me to die.“ / And he sat down somewhere; / And the LORD God prepared a gourd, / to be him a shadow; … And Jonah was exceeding glad, / but God prepared a worm, / so that the gourd withered away. / Therefore Jonah fainted. … „It is better for me to die.“ / Then said the LORD to him: / Thou hast had pity on the gourd, / the which thou hast not made; … And should I not spare Nineveh, / many thousand persons, / who cannot discern left from right, / and also much cattle?

O LORD our Lord, how excellent / is thy name in all the / earth! who hast set thy glory a-bove the heavens. Prophet … Zechariah saw the angel / of the LORD, Christ riding / on a red horse and he stood a-mong the myrtle trees and … spake with him. Christ is the branch, the / stone with seven eyes, who / removed the iniquity of / that land in one day. He … hath built the temple of the LORD; / and sits and rules upon / his throne; and he is also a / priest: and the counsel of … peace is between them both. Daniel / saw Christ clothed in linen, / whose loins were girded with fine gold / of Uphaz: His body … also was like the beryl, and / his face as the appea-rance of lightning, and his eyes as / lamps of fire, and his … arms and his feet like in colour / to polished brass, and the / voice of his words like the voice of / a multitude. Christ was … with Daniel's friends in the burning / fi'ry furnace his form / was like the Son of God. Eli-akim is a type of … Christ, the key of the house of Da-vid is laid upon his / shoulder; he openeth, and none / shall shut; and he shutteth, … and none shall open. They that are / far off have come and build / in the temple of the LORD as / Zechariah proph'sied. … It was not day, nor night: but it / came to pass, that at e-vening time it became light. And / half of the city of … Jerusalem went forth into / captivity, and the / residue of the people was / not cut off from t'city. … Christ is the wisdom which the LORD / possessed in the begin-ning of his way, before his works / of old. All proverbs of … Solomon are given from one / shepherd, Jesus Christ. Ma-ny people go and say, Come ye, / and let us go up to … the mountain of the LORD, to the / house of the God of Ja-cob; and he will teach us of his / ways, and we will walk in … his paths: for out of Zion went / forth the law, and the word / of the LORD from Jerusalem. / Christ judgeth among the … nations, and rebuketh many / people: and we have bea-ten our swords into plowshares, / and our spears into … pruninghooks: nation doth not lift / up sword against nation, / neither do we learn war any / more. O house of Jacob, ... come ye, and let us walk in the / light of the LORD.

160 Matthew

O LORD our Father, how excel-lent is thy name in all / the earth! and the name of thy Son / Jesus Christ who came to ... us through Mary begotten of / the Holy Spirit in / Bethlehem in the days of He-rod the king as written ... by the prophet, And thou Bethle-hem, in the land of Ju-dah, art not the least among the / princes of Judah: for ... out of thee shall come a Gover-nor, that shall rule my peo-ple Israel. The wise men saw / the star of the King of ... the Jews and worshipped him and pre-sented unto him gifts. / Herod sought to destroy the child / and they fled to Egypt ... that it might be fulfilled which was / spoken of the Lord by / the prophet, saying, Out of E-gypt have I called my son. ... And Herod slew the children as / prophesied. Jospeh came / to Nazareth as prophesied. / And John baptized Jesus ... and he saw the Spirit of God / descending like a dove, / and lighting upon him: And lo / a voice from heav'n, saying, ... This is my beloved Son, in / whom I am well pleased. Then / was Jesus led up of the Spi-rit to the wilderness ... to be tempted of the devil, / but Jesus withstood him. / And he came to Capernaum, / there in the borders of ... Zabulon and Nephthalim: That / it might be fulfilled which / was spoken by the prophet, that / the people saw great light. ... Jesus preached repentance and Pe-ter and Andrew with James / and John became his disciples. / Jesus healed all manner ... of sickness among the people. / He called Matthew and the / rest of the twelve disciples who / healed likewise and preached the ... kingdom of heaven as Jesus / commanded. Jesus rode / to Jerusalem as prophe-sied, Tell ye the daughter ... of Sion, Behold, thy King com-eth unto thee, meek, and / sitting upon an ass, and a / colt the foal of an ass. ...Jesus spoke at Passah, Take, eat; / this is my body. And / drink ye all of the cup; For this / is my blood of the new … testament, which is shed for ma-ny for the remission / of sins. And Judas betrayed Je-sus for thirty pieces … of silver. And the high priest said / unto him, art thou the / Christ, the Son of God. Jesus saith / unto him, Thou hast said. … Jesus was sentenced but Judas / gave the money back and / they bought with it the potter's field / as Jeremiah spake. … And Jesus came to Golgotha / where they crucified him / and they parted his garments, cas-ting lots as prophesied. … He died and the earth did quake, and / the rocks rent; the veil of / the temple was rent, the graves were / opened; many bodies … of the saints arose and appeared / unto many. The cen-turion, and they that were with / him, feared greatly, saying, … Truly this was the Son of God. / On the third day he rose / again from the dead and at the / grave there was a great earth-quake and an angel appeared. And / Jesus spake unto them, / saying, All power is given / unto me in heaven … and in earth. Go ye therefore, and / teach all nations, bapti-zing them in the name of the Fa-ther, and of the Son, and … of the Holy Ghost: Teaching them / to observe all things what-soever I have commanded / you: and, lo, I am with … you alway, even unto the / end of the world. Amen.

161   **Matthew 4:4**

It is written, Man shall not live / by bread alone, but by / every word that proceedeth out / of the mouth of God. Now … it is high time to awake out / of sleep: for now is my / salvation nearer than when I / believed. Let us therefore … cast off the works of darkness, and / let us put on the ar-mour of light. The Lord Jesus shall / be revealed from heaven … with his mighty angels, In fla-ming fire taking ven-geance. And blessed are they that do / his commandments. Let me … approve things that are excellent; / that I may be sincere / and without offence till the day / of Christ; Some indeed preach … Christ even of envy and strife / which corrupt the word of / God, but I speak as of since-rity, not to please men. … I trust in the living

God. The / ungodly are not wise, / they measure themselves by themselves, / and compare themselves 'mong ... themselves. For all seek their own, not / the things which are Jesus / Christ's. So then because they are luke-warm, Christ will spue them out ... of his mouth. The God of hope fill / you with all joy and peace / in believing, that ye may a-bound in hope, through the pow'r ... of the Holy Ghost. God bless o-ur church!

162   Matthew 5:48

Our Father which art in hea-ven, thou art perfect. Thou / art all-knowing and thou seest / in secret. And thou dost ... abundantly pardon and for-givest transgression. Thou / feedest the fowls of the air, and / givest food to all, thou ... knowest that we have need of all / these things; thou givest good / things to them that ask thee and with-holdest no good thing from ... us. Thou hast the death of sparrows / in thy hands and one of / them shall not fall on the ground with-out thee, Father. Thou art ... the Lord of heaven and earth, thou / hidest thyself from the / wise and prudent, and revealest / thyself unto babes. Yea, ... I thank thee, even so, Father: / for so it seemed good in / thy sight. Thou hast delivered all / things unto Christ: and no ... man knoweth thee, save the Son, and / he to whomsoever / the Son will reveal him. Every / plant, which thou hast not plant'd, ... shall be rooted up, all repro-bates shall be judged by the / Son, the Lord Jesus Christ.

163   The Lord's Prayer

Thus our Lord Christ taught us to / pray: Our Father which / art in heaven, Hallow'd be thy / name. Thy kingdom come. Thy ... will be done in earth, as it is / in heaven. Give us this / day our daily bread. And for-give us our debts, as ... we forgive our debtors. And / lead

us not into temp-tation, but deliver us from / evil: For thine is the …
kingdom, and the power, and the / glory, for ev'r. Amen.

164   **Matthew 9:36**

When I see the multitudes, I'm / moved with compassion on / them,
because they faint, and are scat-tered abroad, as sheep which …
have no shepherd. The harvest tru-ly is great, but the la-bourers are
few: O Lord of the / harvest, send forth lab'rers … into thy harvest.
Thus saith the / Lord GOD unto these bones; / Behold, I will cause
breath to en-ter into you, and ye … shall live: And shall put my
spirit / in you, and shall add you / to my church, I will gather you /
to my holy people, … And ye shall know that I am the / LORD, then
shall ye know that / I the LORD have spoken it, and / performed it,
saith the LORD. … Now come ye heathen, come to God, / the
LORD; be converted / and you shall have peace. So come now / to
the Lord and Saviour … Jesus Christ and believe today / upon his
name and ye / shall have salvation. We pray that / utterance may be
giv'n … unto us, that we may open / our mouth boldly, to / make
known the mystery of the / gospel, and to persuade … men to come
to Christ. LORD, give thy / church thy Holy Ghost to / gather lost
souls, to fish men.

165   **Matthew 26:36-46**

My Lord and Saviour Jesus Christ / thou wentest with thy di-sciples
to Gethsemane, and / saidst to the disciples, … Sit ye here, while I
go and pray / yonder. And thou tookest / with thee Peter and the two
sons / of Zebedee, and thou … beganst to be sorrowful and / very
heavy. Then thou / saidst unto them, My soul is ex-ceeding
sorrowful, yea, … even unto death: tarry ye / here, and watch with
me. And / thou wentest a little further, / and fellest on thy face, …
and prayedst, saying, O my Fa-ther, if it be possi-ble, let this cup

pass from me: ne-vertheless not as I … will, but as thou wilt. And thou cam'st / unto the disciples, / and findest them asleep, and saidst / unto Peter, What, could … ye not watch with me one hour? / Watch and pray, that ye en-ter not to temptation: the spi-rit indeed is willing, … but the flesh is weak. Thou wentest / away again the se-cond time, and prayedst, saying, O / my Father, if this cup … may not pass away from me, ex-cept I drink it, thy will / be done. And thou camest and found / them asleep again: for … their eyes were heavy. And thou hast / left them, and wentest a-way again, and prayedst the third / time, saying the same words. … Then thou camest to thy disci-ples, and saidst unto them, / Sleep on now, and take your rest: be-hold, the hour is at … hand, and the Son of man is be-trayed into the hands of / sinners. Rise, let us be going: / behold, he is at hand … that doth betray me.

166   **Matthew 28:19**

I am baptized in the name of / the Father, and of the / Son, and of the Holy Ghost for / the remission of my … sins. I am baptized in the name / of the Lord Jesus, as / Christ and the Apostles comman-ded. And I am baptized … into the death of Christ Jesus / and have confessed my sins / and followed the Lord Jesus in / baptism, my sins are … washed and I am buried in his / death. In baptism I / died with him and as he was raised / from the dead so am I … and I walk in newness of life, / I have been planted to-gether in the likeness of his / death, and so shall I be … also in the likeness of his / resurrection: In the / water my old man was cruci-fied with him, so that the … body of sin might be destroyed, / that henceforth I should not / serve sin. I am dead and therefore / freed from sin. I believe … that I shall also live with Christ, / because Christ lives. In that / I live, I live unto God and / justified God there in … baptism as the answer of / a good conscience toward / God. I am saved as Noah in / the arch, through the water … and am baptized with the Holy /

Ghost and with fire. Through / one baptism we keep the u-nity of the Spirit … in the bond of peace. For by one / Spirit are we all bap-tized into one body, and we / have been all made to drink … into one Spirit. I am cir-cumcised by the circum-cision of Christ in putting off / the body of the sins … of the flesh, with the circumci-sion made without hands and / I'm sure, he that believeth and / is baptized shall be saved.

167   Luke 1:35

We praise thee, O Holy Ghost, who / camest to Maria / and Christ was born through thee. Thou didst / come on him like a dove … from heaven. Thou didst come at Pen-tecost in power on / the disciples in cloven tongues / like as of fire. And … thou didst work many miracles / through the hands of the A-postles and the disciples. Thou / appointest elders and … deacons in churches and givest / gifts to every one as / thou pleasest. Thou art our Com-forter and Advocate, … Holy Ghost, thou art with us and / helpest us always. Thou / guidest us into all truth and / bringest all things to our … remembrance that God hath said and / thou guidest us in great / decisions through promptings and out-ward signs of providence … and thou bearest witness that we / are the children of God. / And thou helpest us in prayer / whereby we cry, Abba, … Father. Thou helpest us to pro-claim Christ to every crea-ture. And thou givest great boldness / and comest sent by the … Father and by Christ, thou art God / thyself and thou glori-fiest the Son of God. And through / thee the Scriptures hath been … written and thou speakest to us / through the Word and givest / us firy fervor in the ser-vice of God. And we plead … thee Father, may Christ baptize ma-ny with the Holy Ghost / through the preaching of the gospel.

Blessed is he who putteth his / hand to the plough, and doth / not look back. I suffer long, and / am kind; I envy not; … I vaunt not myself, and am not / puffed up, I do not be-have myself unseemly, I seek / not my own, I am not … easily provoked, I think no / evil; I rejoice not / in iniquity, but rejoice / in the truth; I bear all … things, and believe all things, I hope / all things, endure all things. / I covet earnestly the best / gifts. On my forehead it … is written: Holiness to the / LORD. My life is a sa-crifice to God for a sweetsmel-ling savour. I'm salted … with fire and the sufferings / of Christ abound in me / and I eat bitter Passah-herbs. / I bear his reproach there … without the camp. Sin is conta-gious but righteousness not, / therefore no sinners dwell with me. / The nations murder their … babies in the womb, mothers mur-der their children before / they are born. The Evangeli-cals and Catholics bear … still the blood upon them in all / the world until judgment-day. They marry man with man and / female with female in … the church. All men go into the / private brothel on the / internet and it is not banned. / Women run on the streets … exposed, the world is ripe for slaugh-ter. And they live in loose / relationships and beget il-legitimate children … and many are divorced. They use / contraceptives and do / not keep their virginity, and / they explain away the … Bible and adjust the doctrine / to the desires of / men. They do not preach clearly and / do not name the sins. Help, … O LORD, and keep us pure!

169　　　Acts

Give ear, O my people, to my / law: incline your ears to / the words of my mouth. Which we have / heard and known, and our … fathers have told us. We will not / hide them from their children, / shewing to the generation / to come the praises of … the LORD, and his strength, and his won-derful works that he hath / done. At Pentecost the Holy / Ghost came and they spoke in … strange tongues and Peter preached the word. / Three thousand were saved. The / Apostles worked signs and wonders / and were persecuted … by the council. Stephen was stoned / and Samaria re-ceived the word; Saul of Tarsus was / miraculously saved. … Tabitha was raised from the dead; / the word went forth to the / heathen in Joppa and further / to Antioch. And King … Herod persecuted the church / and murdered James and put / Peter into prison. But Pe-ter was freed by n'angel … and Herod died by the hand of / an angel. Paul and Bar-nabas travelled to Zyprus and / to Pisidia and … they came to Iconium; they / preached boldly in the Lord / and worked signs and wonders. They came / to Derbe and Lystra … and healed a man impotent in / his feet. They came through Phry-gia and Mysia and Ti-mothy came to them. The …churches increased in number dai-ly. They came to Maze-donia as they were called by / the Lord. They stayed there in … Philippi and the house of Ly-dia was baptized and / also the house of the jailor. / They preached always under … persecution and in Thessa-lonica a great mul-titude was added. Paul and Si-las went to Berea … and through Athens Paul came to the / Corinthians. In this / city the Lord has much people / and Paul convinced many … and travelled to Ephesus. He / went back to Jerusa-lem and came back to Ephesus / and the word of God grew … mightily and prevailed. After / much traveling he came / back to Jerusalem and was / taken captive by the … Jews. He suffered shipwreck at Mal-ta and was brought to Rome. / There he was a captive but still / preached.

170   1 Corinthians 11:13

Is it comely that a woman / pray unto God unco-vered? Shall she approach the throne of / the almighty bare? Which … spirit is in the sight of God / of great price? It is a / chaste conversation coupled with / fear. They shall be pure in … godliness and the adorning / not the outward of plai-ting the hair, and of wearing of / gold, or of putting on … of apparel; But let it be / the hidden man of the / heart, not as Isebel who put / paint on her eyes. Not as … the whore who paints the eyes, but as / Rebeccah who covered / herself before Isaac. Yea, / they shall pray to God in … modest apparel, with shamefac-edness and sobri'ty / they shall approach the throne of the / LORD. As becom'th women … professing godliness as la-dies adorned with good works, / in subjection to their own hus-bands with a meek and quiet … spirit that the prayers be not / hindered. LORD, look at our / prayers and hear our cries as we / approach thee with fear!

171   Ephesians 2

Praise ye the LORD from the heavens, / for by grace are we saved / through faith; and that not of ourselves: / it is the gift of God: … Not of works, lest any man should / boast. Our Lord is great / in counsel, and mighty in work. / The Lord Jesus Christ is … the second Adam made for our / redemption. Blessed are / the poor in spirit: for theirs is / the kingdom of heaven. … Blessed are they that mourn: for they / shall be comforted. Bless'd / are the meek: for they shall inhe-rit the earth. Blessed are … they which do hunger and thirst af-ter righteousness: for they / shall be filled. Bless'd are the merci-ful: for they shall obtain … mercy. Blessed are the pure in / heart: for they shall see God. / Blessed are the peacemakers: for / they shall be called children … of God. Blessed are they which are / persecuted for righ-teousness' sake: for theirs is the king-dom of heaven. Praise ye … the LORD.

172   Colossians 1

We thank thee God and Father of / our Lord Jesus Christ / that we have heard of the word of / the truth of the gospel. … We do not cease to pray and to / desire that we might / be filled with the knowledge of thy / will in all wisdom and ... spiritu'l understanding; That / we might walk worthy of / the Lord unto all pleasing, be-ing fruitful in every ... good work, and increasing in the / knowledge of God; Strengthened / with all might, according to his / glorious power, to ... all patience and longsuffering / with joyfulness; Giving / thanks unto thee our Father, / who hast made us meet to ... be partakers of the inhe-ritance of the saints in / light: Who hast delivered us from / the power of darkness, ... and hast translated us into / the kingdom of thy dear / Son: In whom we have redemption / through his blood, even the ... forgiveness of sins: Who is the / image of the invi-sible God, the firstborn of e-very creature: For by him ... were all things created, that are / in heaven, and that are / in earth, visible and invi-sible, whether they be ... thrones, or dominions, or princi-palities, or powers: / all things were created by him, / and for him: And he is ... before all things, and by him all / things consist. And he is / the head of the body, the church: / who is the beginning, ... the firstborn from the dead; that in / all things he might have the / preeminence. For it pleased the / Father that in him should ... all fulness dwell.

173   **1 Timothy 2:1-10**

Our LORD God, thou hast comman-ded us to meet as a / church to pray. The Apostles with / the early church met in ... the upper room to plead. As prea-ching was forbidden to / the early church they met to pray / as thy word saith. If two ... of you shall agree on earth as / touching any thing that / they shall ask, it shall be done for / them of the Father which ... is in heaven. For where two or / three are gathered toge-ther in Christ's name, there he is in / the midst of us. Thou hast ... said the prayer meeting is im-portant before all things, / first of all stands the church's pray-er meeting. We gather ... first and foremost to ask of thee, / as thou commandest. So / hear us, O LORD, as we gather / in thy name, hear our prayer … as we cry unto thee O God! / Men, come without wrath and / doubting, women in modest ap-parel. Then our LORD … God will hear, yea, thou wiltst hear us / when we come to pray in / the name of Christ.

174   1 Timothy 3:1-7; Titus 1:6-9

If a man desire the of-fice of a bishop, he / desireth a good work. A bi-shop then must be blameless, … the husband of one wife, he is / the steward of God; not / selfwilled, a pastor is not soon / angry, he is just and … holy, temp'rate, a lover of / good men, vigilant, so-ber, of good behaviour, given / to hospitality, … apt to teach; Not given to wine, / no striker, not greedy / of filthy lucre; but patient, / not a brawler, and not … covetous; One that ruleth well / his own house, having his / children in subjection with all / gravity; yea, faithful … children not accused of riot / or unruly (For if / a man know not how to rule his / own house, how shall he take … care of the church of God?) Not a / novice, lest being lif-ted up with pride he fall into / the condemnation of … the devil. Moreover he must / have a good report of / them which are without; lest he fall / into reproach and the … snare of the devil. Holding fast / the faithful word as he / hath been taught, that he may be a-ble by sound doctrine both … to exhort and to convince the / gainsayers. Ordain such / elders as it is commanded / to you.

175   2 Timothy 3:1-5

These last days are perilous times. / For men are lovers of / their own selves, covetous, boasters, / proud, blasphemers, and are … disobedient to parents, / unthankful, unholy, / Without nat'ral affection, truce-breakers, false accusers, … incontinent, fierce, despisers / of those that are good, and / Traitors, heady, highminded, lo-vers of pleasures more than … lovers of God; Having a form / of godliness, but de-nying the power thereof: from / such turn away. For God … gave them over to a repro-bate mind, to do those things / which are not convenient; and / the ungodly are filled … with all unrighteousness, forni-cation, wickedness, co-vetousness, maliciousness; full / of envy, murder, d'bate, … deceit, malignity; whispe-rers, Backbiters, haters / of God, despiteful, inventors / of evil things, Without … understanding, covenantbrea-kers, implacable, un-merciful: knowing the judgment / of God, that they're worthy … of death. They are full of adul-tery, uncleanness, las-civi'sness, idolatry, witch-craft, hatred, variance, … emulations, wrath, strife, sedi-tions, heresies, envy-ings, drunkenness, revellings, and / such like. They are fearful, … unbelieving, abomina-ble, whoremongers, sorce-rers, they love and make lies. They are / thiefs, they bear false witness, … have evil eyes and follow the / beast of the sea, they are / roman-catholic and follow / the beast of the earth, the … evangelical and reformed / church. The sins of these chur-ches have reached unto heaven, and / God remembereth her … iniquities. These both will be / cast alive into a / lake of fire burning with brim-stone. Blessed are they that … do his commandments, that they may / have right to the tree of / life, and may enter in through the / gates into the city. … Blessed are they who by patient / continuance in well / doing seek for glory, honour / and immortality. … I will glory in the Lord and / am not wise in my own / conceit. I am kindly affec-tioned to my brethren with … brotherly love. I abhor that / which is evil and cleave / to that which is good. I am not / slothful in business; but … continuing instant in pray'r; / I am given to hos-pitality, serving the Lord. / I recompense to no … man evil for evil. Remem-ber me, O my God, con-cerning this, and wipe not out my / good deeds that I have done … for the house of my God, and for / the offices thereof. / I trust thee with childlike faith and / keep the simplicity … that is in Christ. I cause no di-visions and give no of-fense and look after the weak con-sciences, and I hate the … Nicolaitans as thou hast / commanded. I hold the / traditions of the Apostles. / Remember me, O my … God, concerning this also, and / spare me according to / the greatness of thy mercy. Thou, / O LORD rewardest me ... according to my righteousness; / according to the clean-ness of my hands doest thou re-compense me. For I love ... my enemies, and bless them that / curse me, and do good to / them that hate me, and pray for them / which despitefully use ... me, and persecute me; And thou / hast shined in my heart, and / given the light of the knowledge / of the glory of God ... in the face of Jesus Christ. Thou / hast blessed me with all spi-ritu'l blessings in heavenly / places in Christ: Father ... thou hast chosen me in him be-fore the foundation of / the world, that I should be holy / and without blame before ... thee in love: And thou hast predes-tinated me unto / the adoption of children by / Jesus Christ to thyself, ... according to the good pleasure / of thy will, To the praise / of the glory of thy grace, O / God, wherein thou hast made ... me accepted in the belo-ved. In whom we have re-demption through his blood, the forgive-ness of sins, according ... to the riches of his grace. To / thee be glory for e-ver and ever. Amen.

176   1 Peter 2:6

The LORD hath founded the church on / Jesus Christ the chief cor-ner stone, blessed is he that takes / refuge in him and woe ... to them wich stumble at him. His / voice breaketh the cedars / and in his temple doth every / one speak of his glory. ... Let all the inhabitants of / the world stand in awe of / him, even so, Lord of hosts, for / so it seemeth good in ... thy sight. Jesus Christ ruleth in / the church in truth and right-teousness is his royal garment. / On his head are many ... crowns; and he hath a name written, / that no man knows, but he / himself. True and righteous are his / judgments, and he is our ... mighty fortress, our hiding place / and shield. In his church we / shout for joy, he sitteth high and / lifted up at the right ... hand of the Father of glory. / His gospel giveth hope / to all nations, yea, Jesus Christ / is our only hope. … For there is none other name un-der heaven given a-mong men, whereby we must be saved. / We come boldly unto … the throne of grace, that we may ob-tain mercy, and find grace / to help in time of need. Kings of / all the earth are in thy … kingdom, Lord Jesus Christ and thou / hast made us kings and priests / a people of thy favour as / prophesied. Everything … did come to pass and was wonder-fully fulfilled in these / last days, O Lord of hosts. We thank / thee heartily and we … rejoice in thy name for ever / and ever. Amen.

177   1 John 5:7

Praise ye the LORD. Praise the name of / the Father, the Word, and / the Holy Ghost: For these three bear / record in heaven, and … these three are one. God is one and / his essence is undi-vided. He is love, he is light / his essence is simple … and without parts. Praise the LORD, for / he sent Christ our scapegoat / into the wilderness! Our Josh-ua leads us into … the land of Cana'n. Out of E-zekiel's temple run-neth water into the sea and / the waters are healed. Yea, … every thing that liveth, which mo-veth, whithersoever the / rivers come, liveth. The trees there / bring forth new fruit 'ccording … to their months, and the leaf thereof / are for medicine. Blessed / is the church wherein no leaven / is found. Blessed are those … who consecrate themselves as Na-zarites. The LORD delights / in those who serve mornings and e-venings in the temple, … who always fill the lamps with oil / and enlighten them. Ho-ly Church, praise ye the LORD; ye Chris-tians, praise your God! For he … giveth you food and raiment of-fer him for this the shew-bread! Shout for joy, come with harps and / play unto the LORD with … thanksgiving! Build the taberna-cle, build the church wherein / the glory of God dwelleth! Add / nothing to it and take … nothing away from it, do e-verything as commanded! / Praise him all ye angels! Christ was / offered on the great day … of atonement. He is our ci-ty of refuge

whereto / we flee. The arc of God's cove-nant is in our church …
and he communes with us from there. / The mercy seat covers / o'r
sins. O'r Boas hath redeemed / us. The LORD hath written … his
law on our heart. Ye Chris-tians, praise the LORD!

178   **Revelation 1:9-20**

Who is there among the golden / candlesticks? One like un-to the
Son of man, clothed with a / garment down to the foot, … and girt
about the paps with a / golden girdle. His head / and his hairs were
white like wool, as / white as snow; and his eyes … were as a flame
of fire; And / his feet like unto fine / brass, as if they burned in a furnace; and his voice as the … sound of many waters. And he / had in
his right hand sev'n / stars: and out of his mouth went a / sharp
twoedged sword: and … his countenance was as the sun / shineth in
his strength. I / am the first and the last: I am / he that liveth, and
was … dead; and, behold, I am alive / for evermore, Amen; / and
have the keys of hell and of / death. It is Christ, the Lord, … the
twoedged sword is his word, / piercing even to the / dividing
asunder of soul / and spirit, and of the … joints and marrow; the
golden can-dlesticks are churches and / the stars are pastors. The
Lord is / among the churches and … hath the pastors in his hand.

179   **Revelation 5:13**

Blessing, and honour, and glory, / and power, be unto / him that
sitteth upon the throne, / and unto the Lamb for … ever and ever.
Amen. Je-sus Christ, the Son of man / is come to seek and to save
that / which was lost. Whosoev'r … shall confess him before men,
him / will he confess also / before his Father which is in / heaven.
But whosoev'r … shall deny Christ before men, him / will he also
deny / before his Father which is in / heaven. He is not come … to
send peace on earth: He came not / to send peace, but a sword. / For

he is come to set a man / at variance against … his father, and the daughter a-gainst her mother, and the / daughter in law against her mo-ther in law. And a man's … foes shall be they of his own house-hold. He that loveth fa-ther or mother more than me is / not worthy of me: and … he that loveth son or daughter / more than me is not wor-thy of me. And he that taketh / not his cross, and follow'th … after me, is not worthy of / me. Jesus Christ saith: Come / unto me, all ye that labour / and are heavy laden, … and I will give you rest. Take my / yoke upon you, and learn / of me; for I am meek and low-ly in heart: and ye shall … find rest unto your souls. We are / the salt of the earth and / the light of the world. We let o-ur light so shine before … men, that they see our good works, / and glorify our / Father which is in heaven in / the day of vis'tation. … I strive to enter in at the / strait gate: for many will / seek to enter in, and they shall / not be able. For the … righteous will scarcely be saved, there-fore I forsake all that / I have to be a disciple. / I love Jesus Christ, and … keep his words: and the Father lo-veth me, and they came un-to me, and they made their abode / with me. The Holy Ghost … teacheth me all things and bringeth / all things to my remem-brance, whatsoever Christ hath said. / I keep his commandments … and abide in his love. Christ's joy / remaineth in me, and / my joy is full. I love all the / brethren. The world hateth … me, as it hated Christ before / it hated me. The world / hateth me because Christ hath cho-sen me out of the world … and because I am not of the / world anymore. I have / received Christ's word and believed on / him and am now his.

180

According to Ausbund 44, a song of George Simons, sentenced in the Netherlands, 1557.

Hear ye peoples what I want to / tell you, hold the word of / God sharply before your children, / this is a good treasure. … Live accordingly and give a / good example and God / be praised. George Simons wrote his son / in his distress, because … they intended to kill him in / Harlem. He was impri-soned for the truth's sake and writes these / things unto you. He said, … my son, incline thine ear unto / my words, be obedient / and turn from evil. Have God always before thine eyes in … all thy life and be not inte-rested in the world. If / God showeth you his will, do it / speedily. Be only … with the righteous and avoid the / proud boys. Remember that / we have to answer in judgment / for all our works. Do … not live according to the flesh / and self-will, but only / according to God's will. Those who / live after the flesh are … living dead. God is with those who / mortify the deeds of / the flesh. The carnal mind is enmity against God and … therefore the rich man is in the / flames. Read the scriptures and / make a diff'rence between the doc-trine of God and of men. … This is my heart's desire that / thou comest not into / the pains of the ungodly, whom / the godly hate. Fifteen-fifty-seven they put George Si-mons at the stake. Take it / to heart ye parents and give a / good example to your … children, that they may see only / good fruit in you. Blessed / be the Lord! Amen.

181

According to Ausbund 45; a new spiritual song, wherein a disciple of Christ laments that afflictions have met him for the word's sake: the Lord answered him meekly with an explanation of how his life in this world was; of Hans Büchel, written in prison in Passau, 1535-40.

It was in the time when I was / cast out, I did sink in-to deep sorrow because I had / to leave wife and children. / It rained much and it was windy / and I went on that way / and told God my sorrow that he / might not leave me. I sighed … and wept. O highest Maker, thou / hast given me a wife / and little children that I may / nourish them, but now the … magistrates do not allow me / and that hurts beyond mea-sure. I have committed no crime, / but I received answer: / The foxes have holes, and the birds / of the air have nests; but / the Son of man hath not where to / lay his head. Christ, the Lord, … saith: I have to suffer vi'lence / from Jews and heathen and / they did cast a lot for my gar-ment, they made me naked … and bare. I have received a let-ter that I need to go / to prison as if I had com-mitted a murder. They … spit at me and crucified me / and put a crown of thorns / on my head. They gave me vine-gar and gall to drink and … said: Art thou God, then step down from / the cross. They call me an / enthusiast and a dreamer, / I must be a devil. … If I separate myself from / evil they say I crawl / into the corners. He who fol-low'th me will have the same … fate as I had. The pastors say / this people needs to be / blotted out with the sword. They count / me among t'murderers, … Barabbas was freed, but I was / crucified. O God! Who / may declare thy fervent love? A / heart might break that they have … been so hard against thee and thou / art still so gracious. Lord / give me patience and forgive the / sin of all who hate me. … I could say much to thee, but I / cannot. I went into / a wood and wept bitterly. Lord / protect my wife and my … children. O God, I have faith.

182

According to Ausbund 46; a new spiritual song of these horrible last days wherein are so many sects and false prophets with bloodthirsty tyrants; of Hans Büchel, written in prison in Passau, 1535-40.

These are dang'rous times as were ne-ver heard since God made the / heavens and the earth. Princes rule / the spiritual sword, … as the false prophets teach them and / the godly don't know where / to go. All sins that one can think / of are now normal and … all praise themselves as a church of / God. The Turks, Jews, Heathen, / Pope, Luther and other sects which / I do not want to talk … about, every one wants to be / right. One people hates the / other, O God, look at it! Save / thine elect! My int'mates … have betrayed me, O Lord, forgive / them! In Worms the high-priests / and the scribes take counsel in the / fifty-seventh year that … all might be sentenced by sword who / teach something against them. / And he who doth not want to go / to church must go to pris'n … and be tormented until they / recount. Who hath heard such / a thing, that Christians be conver-ted to the kingdom of … God by the sword? Be patient, thou / O pious Christian and / feed thy enemies meekly and / be merciful to all … as thy Father in heaven doth! / Keep thyself pure and chaste / and abstain from all appearance / of evil and let your … moderation be known unto / all men. What you want that / do to others. Take the right mea-sure in everything and … love thine enemy heartily / that curse thee. Give him coun-sel and lend him, therein a friend / of the Lord is known. O … world, thy communion and thy bap-tisms are in vain if / thou keepest not the commandments! / What for do you run to … church? You live as the heathen with / usury and blasphe-my, greed, gambling, gluttony, drin-king, pride, adultery, … idolatry, word-fight, lying / and betraying. The Chris-tians they cast out and give them no-thing to eat, no shelter. … And he who is caught must go with / high penalty to pri-son. It were better for him that / a millstone were hanged ' bout …his neck, and that he were drowned in / the depth of the sea. It / would be better for him who gi-veth offense here to the … innocent if he had not been / born. For God will avenge / the blood of his witnesses in / his wrath. Christ saith, I was … an hungred and thirsty, naked, / sick and in prison, and / ye gave me no meat, and clothed me / or visited me not. … Depart from me, ye that work in-iquity into e-verlasting fire! Come, ye bles-sed of my Father, and … inherit the kingdom of my / Father and rejoice for / evermore! For you have shown me / love and suffered with me. … Therefore think on this ye rulers / and ye subjects, ye rich / and poor, that ye have mercy on / your neighbors. Be convert'd … heartily and the whole heaven-ly host will rejoice with / thee. May God help us all, Amen.

183

According to different Ausbund-Stanzas: 69 St. 1 + 17 + 21, 50 St. 13, 54 St. 22, 66 St. 18, 68 St. 13 + 16, 71 St. 8-11, 72 St. 2-10.

I want to sing to the glory / of God that they may turn / to the right way. Christ spake about / this time, the princes and … lords have turned from the truth and he / who telleth it to them / will be killed first. They will be ha-ted by everyone and … many die innocently as / o'r Lord Jesus Christ. And / the scribes and Pharao praise them-selves Christians and are not, … one knoweth them by their fruit. The / Scriptures teach in simpli-city the way to salvation / and not one worldly-wise … person hits their content. Luther / saith that God commands e-verything that he wants us to do. / Now I ask the learned … where infant-baptism is taught? / They say Christ is in the / wine and the bread and he who de-nieth it, he will be … beheaded or burnt. The head of / the beast of the sea is / wounded by the evangeli-cal doctrine. The beast of … the earth exerciseth all the / power of the first beast / with coercion and doctrines of / men. It cometh with two … horns as a lamb - and now they are / two - the new pope and the / old. The firy pit is prepared / for the beast and for those … who follow it. Their number is / as the sand on the sea, / the false prophet with his host. The / beast will suffer as those … who are deceived by it, they shall / never have rest. And the / Evangelicals force me to / take their faith and call them … brethren, but they are the whore of / Babylon. She maketh / you drink from her cup of sin and / deceiveth you. Luc'fer … is your ruler and he sendeth / his prophets into all / the countries to corrupt the word / and to kill Christians. The … Roman tyrants wiped out Christians / after the Apostles / until Antichrist came in all / places. And he hath all … earthly treasures in his hand and / giveth them unto his / servants and the poor Christian suf-fereth hunger, and is … persecuted and burnt. The rich / Micah sitteth at ease / and hath ordered his priest who prea-cheth what he desireth. … The teacher hath his food and gar-ment and the temple is / built. Thus the rich followeth his / teaching and trusteth on … the idols. The prophets of the / Antichrist eat from the / table of Isebel and he / who doth not worship their … painted image will be perse-cuted in wrath, but they / shall drown as Pharao's host. When / a Christian cometh the … learned withstand him and call him / a destroyer of Is-rael. Everywhere are false pro-phets and they say Christ is … here and there. They speak peace, peace, but / there is no peace. And God / sends his plagues. I beseech here all / preachers and rulers that … they repent and take an exam-ple of other countries. / God hath made them an end if they / have abased men of God. … Every one shall turn to Christ, he / hath already often / warned us with death, war and famine. / If you will not leave your … sins and will not know Christ, then you / will be drowned in the sea, / you who call yourselves Christians. A-men.

184

According to different Ausbund-Stanzas: 76 St. 1 + 4, 91 St. 10-12, 108 St. 11, 98 St. 6 + 8, 100 St. 12, 103 St. 15, 106 St. 24, 110 St. 2-3, 121 St. 1.

Where should I go in all my dis-tress? God will be my hel-per! Thou wilt not forsake me. They / chide me a Cathar, 'cause … I love the word of God. He that / committeth sin is of / the devil and doth his works and / will be thrown into the … everlasting torments of hell. / The devil sinneth from / the beginning and is the fa-ther of lies. All those that … are deceived by sin, are his chil-dren. A child of God doth / not commit sin, they have cruci-fied their flesh. Whosoev'r … is born of God doth not commit / sin; for his seed remain'th / in him. He who hath baptism / is planted in Christ's death, … all his affection is cruci-fied and he is born a-gain. Christ saith, yea, the time cometh, / that whosoever kill'th … you will think that he doeth God / service. Rejoice if the / world hateth you!

Remember how / she hated me before … you and how they killed the prophets. / Ye children of God, let / us confess the word of God with / our blood! Ye Christians, … ye have known the son of perdition, the Antichrist. The / apostasy hath come and ma-ny deceivers are on … earth. Hear the voices of the souls / under the altar, How / long, O Lord, holy and true, dost / thou not judge and avenge … our blood on them that dwell on / the earth? The Lord saith: rest / yet for a little season till / all your fellowservants … are added, then I will avenge / you. He who doth not leave / house, field, wife, child and hates his life / will not find the kingdom … of God. Christ saith this that we may / be at ease and peaceful / that we break with o'r own will. To / be poor in spirit means … to be at ease. May God be with / us that we may stay his / witnesses in all distresses / until death and that we … may not depart from him.

185

According to Ausbund 102.

The Antichrist sitteth on God's / stead and giveth command-ments according to his will and / saith he who obeyeth … not sinneth. Paul saith, that he ma-keth himself God. And he / who doth not believe him will be / thrown out of the country … or killed. He twists the commandments / of God and comes with great / splendor and they have to bow be-fore him. The Antichrist … forbidd'th to marry, and comman-deth to abstain from meats, / which God hath created to be / received with thanksgiving. … The Antichrist speaketh he for-giveth sins if they con-fess them to him. And to him who / eats the idol-bread of … the priest, he confirms them eter-nal rest. He also say'th / that Christ is in the bread, but he / is not, because Christ com'th … as a lightning from heaven. The / Antichrist buildeth a / beautiful church with gold and puts / his god and his imag's … in it, out of wood, stone, gold and / silver. But God saith, cur-sed is he who maketh an i-mage. God doth not dwell in … temples made with hands, no one hath / ever seen him. He doth / not let water be water, but / he sanctifieth it … to wash the child from origi-nal sin, although it doth / not believe, he baptizeth it, / otherwise it would be … damned. If he smeareth it with chri-sm in the filthy bath / it will be taken into the / kingdom of God, as if … God could not do it otherwise. / The Antichrist and all / who obey him will be thrown in-to the everlasting … fire, Amen.

186

According to Ausbund 105.

I would like to sing and be hap-py, but to no avail. / I am in distress and wait un-til my Comforter com'th. … I am in deep sorrow and have / no joy and only the / Lord can give it back to me. I / wait on the Lord, grant me … patience in this time, that I may / not transgress in my sor-row. I am shattered that I might / despair. That which I have … long confessed is put before my / mind. It wants to afflict / my conscience, although there is no / sin. The affliction is … so hard upon me and it wants / to make me stumble. But / my sin is washed, why am I trou-bled by that which I have … regretted? But thy word saith that / the affliction is a / trial and we shall be refined / by much suffering so … that I may be found as gold. The / deceiver cometh as / an angel cunningly to cause / confusion. O Lord, keep … my conscience from the devil's de-ceit and lead me into / thy peace! Fight thou against the af-fliction then thou wilt not … suffer anymore but have joy! / I am mere dust and a / flower that withereth, give me / strength as Samson and that … I may slay Goliath. When I / die, give me a white robe! / I tell thee in Christ my Son, if / thou wilt have joy and rise … with him, thou must die and be par-taker of his suff'rings. / Then thou wilt inherit my joy, / my eternal kingdom. …Lord God let me not become a / proverb! Thou wilt give it / to me when thou pleasest. O bles-sed be the Lord for his … mercy, if it be joy or pain, / everything is thy gift, / I thank thee heartily. Amen.

187

According to Ausbund 111.

Lord God, Father in heaven, thy / children lament the dis-tresses on earth. All peoples have / come against us and give … us no secure place. The princes / take counsel how they will / wipe out thy people that thou hast / called for thy honor. We … have been made a spectacle to / all the world, they take from / us possession, child and wife and / want to take our life. … But if we worship the beast, we / get back our possession / and child and wife and also o-ur life. This we do not … want to do in this time, but give / our body in the / hands of men. For it is better / to fall in the hands of … men than to turn from God, for he / giveth life afterwards. / If thou doest what men tell thee, / then thou takest the mark … of the beast and dost worship the / great whore of Babylon. / They blaspheme God in heaven in / all nations, uncount'ble … multitudes and will be thrown in-to the firy pit, but / the sealed are few. The whore of Ba-bylon is drunken with … the blood of the saints, because they / take not the mark of the / beast, and they are not allowed to / buy or sell, as John said. … He who takes the mark will drink the / cup of his indigna-tion; and he shall be tormented / with fire and brimstone … for evermore. He who hath put / his hand on the plough and / doth not look back and reaches out / to the goal which is our … Lord Jesus Christ, him God will raise / on the last day where all / plague is devoured. Christ the Lord / saith, that we shall not fear … them which kill the body, but ra-ther him which is able / to destroy both soul and body / in hell. O Lord God from … heaven send us thy power that / we serve thee not coerced, / but out of free love and that we / keep all thy commandments … and sin not. Send to all

nations / thy light that they might live / with thee! Thy will be done,
Lord, all / glory be unto thee … in all eternity, Amen.